When the E

MW01031755

When the Body Speaks applies Jungian concepts and theories to infant development to demonstrate how archetypal imagery formed in early life can permanently affect a person's psychology.

Drawing from Mara Sidoli's rich clinical observations, the book shows how psychosomatic disturbances originate in the early stages of life through unregulated affects. It links Jung's concepts of the self and the archetypes to the concepts of the primary self as conceptualized by Fordham, as well as incorporating the work of other psychoanalysts such as Bion and Klein.

Lucidly written, *When the Body Speaks* is an important book for professionals and students in the fields of child and adult psychoanalysis and psychotherapy.

Mara Sidoli trained as a child and adult analyst at the Society of Analytical Psychology in London. In 1988 she was appointed Visiting Professor at the University of New Mexico. She has supervised and taught infant observation in London, Italy, and the USA.

When the Body Speaks

The archetypes in the body

Mara Sidoli

Edited by Phyllis Blakemore

First published 2000
by Routledge
11 New Fetter Lane, London EC4P 4EE

Simultaneously published in the USA and Canada
by Taylor & Francis Inc
325 Chestnut Street, 8th Floor, Philadelphia PA 19106

Reprinted 2001
by Brunner-Routledge
27 Church, Road Hove, East Sussex BN3 2FA
29 West 35th Street, New York NY 10001

Brunner-Routledge is an imprint of the Taylor & Francis Group

© 2000 Mara Sidoli

Typeset in Times by Regent Typesetting, London
Printed and bound in Great Britain by TJ International Ltd, Padstow, Cornwall

British Library Cataloguing in Publication Data
A catalogue record for this book is available from the British Library

Library of Congress Cataloging in Publication Data
Sidoli, Mara.
    When the body speaks : the archetypes in the body / Mara Sidoli ; edited by
    Phyllis Blakemore.
        p. cm.
    Includes bibliographical references and index.
        1. Somatization disorder--Etiology. 2. Jungian pyschology. 3. Archetype
    (Psychology) 4. Infant pyschology. I. Blakemore, Phyllis. II. Title.
RC552.S66 S53 2000
616.85´24--dc21
                                                                00-032844
ISBN 0–415–18886–5 (hbk)
ISBN 0–415–18887–3 (pbk)

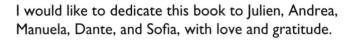

I would like to dedicate this book to Julien, Andrea, Manuela, Dante, and Sofia, with love and gratitude.

Contents

Foreword

The problem of intractable somatic symptoms has been of increasing interest and importance in the analytic field. Without a knowledge of the dynamics of infancy and early childhood, the analyst is limited when it comes to an understanding of the primitive conflicts underlying certain physical illnesses and suicidal impulses. Mara Sidoli and others such as Feldman have looked at how Jung's childhood experience resulted in a split between feeling and intellect that resulted in a gap in his account of early development. From the start, Mara felt drawn to fill this gap, first by translating Michael Fordham's book, *Children as Individuals,* into Italian. Then she moved with her family from Italy to London in order to have an analysis with Fordham and to study his extension of Jung's psychology of the self and archetypes to the realm of infancy and childhood. When Fordham started a training in child analysis at the Society of Analytical Psychology, Mara was one of the first trainees, and then participated in the training as teacher and supervisor. Her area of special interest was mother–baby observation, which she taught in London and later in Santa Fé and New York.

My intention is not to rehearse her career, which was partly that of a pioneer and proselytizer of Fordham's ideas, but to indicate the special gifts that she has brought to the field. In his Preface to her first book, *The Unfolding Self,* Fordham writes that Mara "does not depart into abstract theorizing but uses the theory only as a framework for her entrancing descriptions. How she works with child and adult patients is thus beautifully displayed so that the book is not only technically important but also eminently readable". Those qualities are also to be found in abundance here, with the addition of her mature reflections on the operation of archetypal patterns in earliest infancy, their unfolding in the infant's relationship with the mother, and, drawing on brain research, the way that they become split off and trapped in the body as a result of failures in the early relationship. Her descriptions include dramatic case material and show an unusually gifted clinician at work. Her highly developed intuition, coupled with a robust use of her body and sensation function, enabled her to reach the profoundest levels of disturbance in her patients. There was something of the maverick about her, in that she was not curbed by orthodoxy, and had a maddening disregard for academic and institutional structures. This lack of constriction underlies her profound belief in her own unconscious processes in relation to her patient. Again and again she describes the fantasy that she allows to arise within her, in response both to what the patient tells her and to his or her physical movements. Here she does not rely on theory but on herself for her formulation of the patient's core problem. The theory comes into play only after the patient has been allowed to make a full impact upon her sensibilities. Mara has evolved her own extension of Fordham's theory into the area of the activity of archetypal patterns in the body in earliest infancy, in relation to the instinctual and spiritual poles of the archetype. More controversially, she explores the infantile roots of the collective shadow, drawing closer together a Kleinian and a Jungian understanding of the early damage that can result in psychotic illness.

In her Foreword to J. W. T. Redfearn's book, *My Self, My Many Selves*, Rosemary Gordon has written that one of the factors that attracted her to the Jungian school was the relatively open system of theories, unencumbered by dogmatic beliefs and premature conclusions. She finds that analytical psychology allows space for the individuality of different patients, for the analyst's freedom to find his or her own style of working and for the discoveries of future researchers. Mara's discoveries, as described in this book, range far within that freedom, and sometimes show flashes of genius and magical cure that can excite envy in the reader. They also open extraordinary new vistas.

When the Body Speaks is Mara's summing-up of a career devoted to psychodynamic work, writing, teaching in Europe and the United States, pioneering a new training, supervision, and clinical work. As she herself has said, she ate, breathed, slept, and dreamed analysis, and the fruits of her work are continually growing in the development of her many former students and trainees whose work has been stimulated by her extraordinary energy, great gifts, and love of the work. In the last sentence of the book, she refers to herself as a wounded healer, and her wounds include her treatment for cancer followed by the onset of motor neurone disease. Her study of the conflicts "spoken" in illness is an impressively courageous endeavour, and this book joins the body of work by analytical psychologists and psychoanalysts in a long, difficult progression towards fuller understanding of the psyche–soma.

Miranda Davies
Stroud, February 2000

Acknowledgments

I would like to thank all those who helped make this book possible, especially Phyllis Blakemore, Miranda Davies, Andrew Samuels, Kate Hawes, the *Journal of Analytical Psychology* (JAP), the National Association for the Advancement of Psychoanalysis (NAAP), and all my patients.

Thanks to the Society of Analytic Psychology for permission to reproduce material, versions of which appeared in the *Journal of Analytical Psychology*, 38, 41, and 45.

Introduction

The aim of this book is to synthesize several themes I have developed in the course of my professional life. My main interest has been to link Jung's concepts of the self and instinctual archetypal drives to Michael Fordham's concepts of the primary self and infant development.

Jung's theory of the psyche

Jung conceived of the self as the totality of the psyche, combining the conscious with the unconscious and containing the ego and the archetypes. Paradoxically he also viewed the self as the archetype of order.

The archetypes are organizers of experience, innate predispositions which, although not characterized by that quality of experience which we call consciousness, nonetheless structure and determine the relationship between the internal and external worlds. The archetype in itself is unknowable but is manifested endopsychically and gives rise to typical imagery which has archetypal characteristics. All archetypes are bipolar in that they have a positive or life-enhancing side and a negative or life-destroying side.

Jung defined an archetype as the mental representation of instinctual drives and/or the innate predisposition to experience life according to certain patterns, as well as a powerful way of representing affects.

In Jung's view, affects are the lifeblood of the psyche; perhaps even more significantly, affects are the bridge between body and psyche, instinct and spirit, and influence the psychosoma.

Fordham's theory of the primary self

Michael Fordham understood that Jung's theory of the psyche needed to be applicable to the onset of life and to childhood.

He developed the concept of the "primary self" from Jung's concept of the self. In Fordham's view the primary self represents the totality of the psyche and soma in a germinal state. He conceptualized the primary self as a blueprint, a "steady state of integration" from which the child's ego and bodily growth will unfold through a dynamic process which he termed "deintegration–reintegration" (Fordham 1976).

Fordham postulated that the primary self must deintegrate in order to allow for the dynamic systems (observable soon after birth) to begin to work. The psychic energy bound up in the primary integrate divides into opposites, constellating the opposing archetypal experiences, psychophysiological in nature.

Positive experiences constellate the good aspect of the mother archetype (good breast), and negative experiences constellate the bad aspect of the mother archetype (bad breast).

The integrating experience seems to take place in the following way: as the ego gets stronger, the baby manages to keep within himself the experience of the good breast for increasingly long periods of time and to invoke it in times of need (i.e. in deintegrative phases). Initially the mother's intervention had to be immediate (Fordham 1982). As time goes by, the infant's ego becomes strong enough to substitute the introjected maternal function, in place of the actual mother, in order to bear difficulties with greater ease.

The theory and structure of this book

In addition to the work of Jung and Fordham, my work is also based upon my own observations of early development, as well as material from the most recent studies in the field of infant research on these themes. My particular interest at this stage of my life work is to demonstrate how primary affects contribute to form archetypal imagery and how the archetypal imagery constellated in early life can permanently influence a person's psychology.

Affect-regulation in early life through the intervention of maternal care is essential for healthy psychic development and contributes to a person's ability to self-soothe and self-regulate later in life. Unregulated, untransformed, overwhelming affects triggered in the psychosomatic area activate psychic defense mechanisms such as splitting and denial in order to control violence, destructiveness, and acting out. The strength of these defenses is related to the intensity of the affect that needs containment. Therefore, powerful, rigid defenses are needed to counteract potentially powerful affective outbursts. This very delicate interaction between the developing self and the environmental "mother/culture" is essential to an individual's emotional history.

Many of the patients illustrated in this book have suffered from maternal misattunement and emotional deprivation due to abandonment because of maternal illness or depression. For these infants, the interactive field between their needs and affects and soothing maternal interventions has been out of tune for long stretches of time.

According to Fordham's theory of deintegration and reintegration, it is at times of deintegration of the primary self that an infant absolutely needs the caregiver's attunement. The times the baby feels that his needs have been met must outnumber the times he feels they were unmet, in order to build up the inner experience of being lovable, loved, and safe, and to help him tolerate the swings from good to bad emotional experience-states.

I use clinical material to demonstrate how psychosomatic disturbances are derived from early life stages when the infant's distress messages are not met at an emotional level, and therefore take the route of somatization.

I feel that there is a need in the Jungian literature for this book, not only for therapists and candidates in training, but also for the general reader who wants to understand how Jungian concepts can be applied to early development.

This book fits neither in the classical Jungian stream nor in the object-relations/Kleinian stream. Rather, it fits a more convergent stream, offering a different viewpoint that is of interest to both schools of thought and to all mental health professionals.

Synopsis of chapters

1: Archetypes and birth

In this chapter I discuss the relevance of intrauterine and birth experiences upon subsequent experiences of beginnings in life, in particular the beginning of analysis. I focus on both the personal and collective archetypal constellations surrounding the birth event, as well as on intrapsychic and environmental factors.

2: The little puppet: working with autistic defenses in mother–infant psychotherapy

Here I explore the effects of collective beliefs about child-rearing as well as unconscious parental fantasies and emotions about their developing child. These fantasies shape the archetypal field coloring parental approach to a newborn, thus shaping its destiny.

3: The Jungian infant

The Jungian infant, who lives in an archetypal world, is a fairly new concept. In this chapter I describe the theoretical construct developed to underpin the Jungian Infant Observation Courses I taught. My hypothesis was that, given the fact that an infant's experience is primarily affective, it resides in the psychosomatic realm of the self. This hypothesis was confirmed by actual observation of infants in daily relationships with their mothers. I use case material from these infant observations.

4: Naming the nameless: a way to stop acting out

The ability to communicate with words is a specifically human quality that is slowly developed in the first two years of life. Thus, to be able to use words and language is the first step in the process of symbolization. The use of a shared symbolic code is the only way in which one's personal experiences can be made accessible and transmitted to other human beings. I use cases of two acting-out adolescents.

5: Defense of the self in a case of severe deprivation

This chapter describes the behavior and treatment of a severely disturbed adopted latency boy. Fordham's views of development and Anzieu's concept of psychic envelopes constitute the theoretical underpinning. Bion's concepts of alpha and beta elements are discussed in relation to Jung's views on symbolic development and psychological containment.

6: The shadow: how it develops in childhood

In this chapter I focus specifically on the shadow archetype. My hypothesis is that the material we associate with the shadow pertains to the psychosomatic realm and is shaped by one's earliest infantile experience strictly related to psychosomatic events. My aim is to illustrate the way in which different instinctual discharges from the earliest stage of a person's development tend to constellate typical imagery and fantasies of a powerful and sometimes violent kind. This occurs because of the energetic load typical of the infantile psychosomatic way of experiencing, at a stage when internal and external spaces are not yet felt as differentiated. The chapter is rich in case material.

7: The psychosoma and the archetypal field

I explore here the process by which an individual self, unfolding within the relationship with the maternal object and the cultural matrix, "creates" its internal and external world. I use case material from an infant observation and from the analysis of an adult patient.

8: When the meaning gets lost in the body

This chapter explores severe physical symptoms exhibited by patients at crucial stages of their analyses. With certain patients, when an interpretation manages to break through into a deeply unconscious primitive area, the core of the personality offers extreme resistance, prohibiting infantile contents from acquiring symbolic mental representation. In these patients, a severe somatization occurs. The newly emerging insight appears to be too much for the patient's psyche to deal with.

Conclusion

The conclusion ties together all the important theories of the book.

Chapter 1

Archetypes and birth

Birth is an archetypal event that dramatically influences the environment in which it occurs and, in turn, is dramatically influenced by that environment. Birth has major psychological implications because all human beings have experienced it and therefore have an unconscious mental representation of that experience. This gives rise to a multitude of images related to birth and beginnings. The psyche uses these images in an attempt to depict its own origins, and the way we come into the world has great implications for the way we are going to live and deal with beginnings in life.

All religions and mythologies have creation myths. These myths can be quite fantastic according to the imagination of the people who created them and the environment in which those people lived. The gods in their mythical world have always closely mirrored the culture of the group that worships them. Thus, creation myths and birth rituals have always existed and have provided a meaningful conception of the origins of life.

In our technological world, birth has become a medical event. In the name of progress it has been sterilized of any fantastic or mythic elements. One might say that it has become a sort of illness that needs to be treated in a hospital under medical control.

However, this loss of ritualistic meaning has recently caused our society to rethink the importance of the birthing experience.

From the very beginning of pregnancy, powerful emotions are stirred up in the parents by conscious and unconscious fantasies about the infant. The event of birth evokes highly charged emotional reactions in the newborn's environment because it automatically constellates the fear of death and of life's future potential. It is one of the most profound emotional experiences of life for all those involved, including the newborn. In brief, it stirs up all the fears and anxieties connected with the unknown.

In our culture, the new parents and the professionals involved in the birth are denied psychic space in which to process and work through the emotional experience and their ambivalent feelings about it. Affects possess an energetic charge, and whenever they remain unconscious they can dramatically influence the emotional environment. Where the birth of a child is concerned, one has to pay attention to the presence of powerful affects which may overload the birth field. The extreme anxieties that are stirred up in the new parents and in the professionals involved in the birthing event have to be dealt with and contained. Today's highly technical medical procedures have improved survival standards but have also created a massive barrier of defense mechanisms to prevent emotions from contaminating and taking over the process.

We live in a time when unacknowledged and denied emotional stresses and subtle collective pressures contribute to an accumulation of collective frustration, anger, and resentment in the nuclear families and communities in which members feel deeply alienated from one another. All this tends to interfere dramatically with intimacy within the family and consequently affects the area of parent–child relationships and their emotional stability. In our hectic society, parents have too little time for relating to each other and to their youngsters. Mothers often work full-time outside the home from the start of their infant's life, and an increasing number of fathers are practically unavailable to their children. The pressure of work and the stress of managing the demands of everyday life leave little time for relating, intimacy, and play.

One of the least acknowledged and yet most powerful emotions evoked by the birth of a newborn is envy of the baby, for its intact future, and for the lucky parents who have been blessed with the gift of life.

Therefore, since the origin of humankind, the newborn and his or her parents have usually received ritualized religious blessings as a way of counteracting bad omens and of cathecting hope for the better future the birth brings to the world. This ritualization is exemplified by good auspices and gifts brought by fairies in folk tales, by the kings at the birth of Jesus, and more commonly by gifts brought to newborns and their parents by friends and relatives. All these propitiatory rituals emphasize the importance of welcome and serve to wish a happy beginning to a new member of the group.

Because of the length of pregnancy and the mystery of an unseen presence, birth promotes an extreme sense of expectation. Mixed with curiosity, all sorts of parental fantasies and dreams about the developing infant are stimulated, including predictions about the infant's future and projections of unfulfilled personal potentialities of the parents or the community, including the expectation of the Messiah or Savior.

In my first interview with prospective parents I often am able to picture by their initial transference to me and by my countertransference what sort of welcome they themselves received at birth. I can imagine if they were wanted babies, and whether their birth was a big event or just an uneventful occurrence.

These days the deep emotions that birth evokes in the human psyche are not given sufficient attention. Ambivalent feelings are usually denied by parents rather than explored with the help of supportive family members or professionals. While a great deal of time and energy is spent in creating a safe external environment, the psyches of the parents are neglected. The emotional space in which the baby will be created and shaped by the imagination is often ignored.

Thus, this emotional space is contaminated by polluting elements that are potentially just as lethal to the baby as is the lack of physical care. In Jungian terms we can say that an archetypal field of negative expectations can easily take over and unconsciously condition and contaminate the new birth environment.

All expecting parents experience ambivalent feelings (positive/ negative) about the fetus because, as it grows inside the womb, their fantasies about the baby also begin to grow. In the case of a difficult pregnancy and a risky delivery with a great deal of suffering, it could be expected that a mother might have negative feelings about the destructive power of the baby even before its birth. Thus in her unconscious a negative archetypal field would be constellated, and the infant would acquire the characteristics of the monster baby, with tragic consequences for the attachment process.

The extent to which these fantasies exist is of extreme importance because they influence a healthy relationship between the fetus and its prebirth environment. The expectations and anxieties about the forthcoming event and about the change it will bring and the risks it will entail tend to come up in expectant parents' dreams as well as in their conscious conversation.

After conception and acceptance of the pregnancy, the parents realize that they have no control over what infant is going to be born. This inability to control can create difficulties and in some cases may have extremely negative consequences for their ability to accept the reality of their newborn. They feel they are not able to live "without knowing" and they begin to fantasize about what sort of child they would like to have. If these fantasies are too rigidly determined, they tend to take over the imagination and pre-empt the flow of expectation in their efforts to bring the unknown under control.

There are unfortunately many cases where infants were rejected at birth because of their gender or color or physical imperfection. The parents' rigid expectations will tend to fill up the space where there is an interrelationship between archetypal expectations of the newborn, both positive and negative. This will create a situation where archetypal overdetermined projections from the parents' unconscious will occupy the potential space of the infant–parent relationship. The space will then be filled by unconscious projection, preconceived ideas of what the baby should be like. Thus the natural right of the infant to be himself or herself can be violated even before birth.

Because of his total lack of experience, his unstructured ego, and the extreme intensity of his needs, the infant will tend to induce in the parents highly charged emotional states and responses of a primitive archetypal nature. This means that the parents will often find themselves in quite regressed states, unable to respond to their infant's needs.

Infants have multiple meanings for their mothers and fathers; this creates what infant researchers today define as parental representations of their infants. These theoretical and methodological considerations have arisen from clinical studies. Prenatal fantasies and perceptions of mothers' continuities and changes in the representations of their infants are operative prior to the infant's birth.

Deintegration/reintegration processes

Following Fordham's theory of the primary self, we can say that, for birth to occur both physically and psychologically, a major deintegration has to take place. Not only the infant, but also the mother, the father, and the larger involved community, must experience deintegration, because both physical and emotional space must be made for the baby. One of our major problems as a society is that we do not create this space in the community and tend also to deny the parents time to do it.

Deintegration in the mother

Giving birth is a major emotional as well as physical experience for a woman. In order for this experience to be integrated, the mother's ego/self axis has to undergo a major deintegration. This deintegration, in turn, predisposes her to regress in order to get in touch with the infantile layers of her personality, helping her to empathize with her newborn.

This process of course unsettles the maternal ego. In a normal situation – that is to say when a disintegration does not take place in the mother (post-partum depression or psychosis, for example) – reintegration follows smoothly, re-establishing the ego balance.

The birth event is also disruptive to the relationship of the couple. Just as the woman needs to deintegrate to become a mother, the man has to deintegrate to become a father. This creates a regressive state in the couple that, together with the physical demands of the new baby, gives rise for the first months after birth to a very delicate situation in the family. Hence the family may well need external support to carry on functioning in the world. Usually the situation improves once the reef of the third month is overcome and all the members have managed to survive that difficult time.

During the regressive phase both the mother and father are more easily gripped by archetypal fantasies relating to their own birth experiences and early infancies. These fantasies are coupled with collective archetypal fantasies of the family/community/culture from which the parents originate. To these collective fantasy elements one has to add the medical considerations. Hence, one can easily recognize the complexity of the environment in which an infant is immersed and into which he must adapt in order to survive.

The capacity to adapt is relatively unfamiliar to a baby. In cases where the parents cannot adapt to their newborn, the situation entails complexities and risks.

As if this were not enough, young families have financial pressures. Often a mother must return to work almost immediately after delivery, perhaps before a natural psychological integration has taken place. Thus today we encounter more and more cases of failed attachment and insecure bonding in mother–infant pairs.

From birth to two months, an infant has commonly been thought of as occupying some kind of pre-social, pre-organized, pre-cognitive life phase. Recently, however, some very interesting studies of fetuses (Piontelli 1992) show that a great deal of cognitive and organized behavior goes on in the womb.

Because of this new information, the evaluation of infants' behavior and social life has had to be reconsidered. The baby is born as a highly social being. From the start babies are not always sleeping, eating, fussing, crying, or in full activity. They often occupy a state researchers call "alert inactivity" in which they are physically quiet, yet alert, taking in events with eyes, ears, skin, etc.

The following responses are discernible from birth: head-turning, smelling, non-intensive sucking of fingers or cloth. According to Fordham's theory, these activities would correspond to a low-level de-integration.

I will now give examples from the analyses of patients whose lives were restricted by their own or their parents' rigid archetypal negative unconscious fantasies about birth.

Gene

Gene, a 35-year-old nursery school teacher, came to me because she could not become pregnant. During the course of the analysis we were able to unearth a fantasy in which she equated a fetus with a malignant tumor. Therefore, she could not become pregnant because this would have meant dying of cancer.

At age six, Gene had witnessed her mother die of cancer following the birth of her baby brother. Her child's mind had equated the fetus growing inside the womb with a malignant growth. Although she consciously wished desperately to have a baby, her unconscious terror stopped her from becoming pregnant. After about a year during which we worked through her dreams and her feelings about her early relationship with her mother, her grief for her death, and her hatred of the baby brother, Gene became pregnant. Thanks to the analytic work, a space had been created inside her where a fetus could be differentiated from a malignant tumor.

Gene came regularly twice a week until the birth of a healthy baby boy and then abruptly stopped. She did not want anything else from the therapy. I felt that the bad elements were now projected onto me. She feared that I might want to take her baby away. It seemed to me that she projected onto me her childhood wish to rob her mother of the baby and hence expected that I would become envious and snatch her baby away from her.

Mary

An eight-year-old school-phobic girl named Mary was brought to me for therapy. As soon as I saw her I was struck by an incredibly strong dislike of her physical appearance. I felt this was strange because, although she was not particularly attractive, she was not so ugly either. I began to pay attention to my countertransference. The image of a little monkey came into my mind. It was only several months later that I could make sense of my violent countertransference reaction. Mary said that she had been told that her grandmother had said upon seeing her for the first time,

"What an ugly little monkey." This was a hard projection for Mary to carry; all her life she had felt ugly, unacceptable, and clumsy. Since she had felt forced to come to therapy, she had brought her unconscious fantasy to the first session and had projected the "bad grandmother." Once the fantasy of the monkey was worked through, Mary started to look pretty and felt free to identify with a beautiful princess in her dreams.

Linda

The theme of beauty has been relevant to other female patients who apparently had mothers with preconceived fixed ideas of what a girl should look like.

One patient, a woman in her late forties, came to me because of serious difficulties in relationships. Linda's love relationships were always sadomasochistic. She was plagued by the fact that she did not look like Shirley Temple, her mother's idol. Her mother had done all she could to turn Linda into Shirley Temple. Although she was attractive and intelligent, Linda genuinely believed she was ugly. She felt her mother could not love her, nor could her boyfriends, who regularly hurt and humiliated her.

Lisa

Lisa was a very dark Hispanic woman, born to a very fair Hispanic mother and a dark American Indian/Hispanic father. The mother seems to have rejected Lisa at birth as she found her "black" and could not acknowledge the baby as her own. Lisa, a very interesting and attractive woman, had spent her life feeling ashamed of her skin color. She dreamed of herself as a blonde like Mae West whom her mother greatly admired.

Lisa had to suffer a great deal of humiliation and rejection because she did not correspond to the ideal baby girl of her mother's archetypal dreams. In the transference Lisa continually tried to make me criticize her in a desperate attempt to repeat the past in the present. It was only after she was able to see her mother's hostility and jealousy towards her in relation to an intense father–daughter oedipal bond that Lisa could accept herself and feel free of the curse that had poisoned her life.

There is an absolute need for an infant to be born in a lively emotional and physical environment that is as devoid as possible of rigid predetermined fantasies and expectations on the part of the parents. What an infant needs is to be accepted as he/she is and for the parents to get to know the infant without prejudice. In order for this to happen, the parents must be relatively healthy and in turn must have been welcomed as infants. However, preventive psychoanalytic interventions can help restore a healthy situation.

All the patients described here suffered a terrible narcissistic blow at birth, rather than a warmly enthusiastic welcome. This birth experience reflected negatively on their lives as they seemed to expect rejection and in an uncanny way managed to make this rejection happen. As a result they experienced loss of self-esteem due to self-denigration.

Chapter 2

The little puppet

Working with autistic defenses in mother–infant psychotherapy

Introduction: our society's denial of emotional time and space

In this chapter I should like to explore the effects on a small family of collective beliefs about child-rearing, as well as the effect of unconscious parental fantasies and feelings about their developing child, that is to say, the archetypal field that colors the parental approach to a newborn and shapes its destiny.

As I described in the previous chapter, powerful emotions are stirred up in the parents by conscious and unconscious fantasies about their newborn. In our society there is little to contain these powerful affects and provide a collective method of understanding and working through them.

Another difficulty that contributes to present-day difficulties is that families move around in response to the job market, ignoring the emotional consequences of a relocation away from family ties. In the case of a pregnant woman, this may create high levels of distress for the mother and the new baby and a serious emotional crisis for the new parents.

However, these issues and many others that have their roots in our emotional lives are generally tackled in a concrete way by our culture; people are offered practical advice and solutions which may ease the pain. Instead of making sense of psychic pain we are used to disposing of it as soon as possible with painkillers or other forms of comforting distractions, food, drink, shopping, and so on. Doctors and other members of the helping professions have no time and space in their routine to deal with their own or their patients' psychic pain. Besides, they are not trained to pay attention to emotional distress in their patients. Thus, patients who need to be supported and understood emotionally, like Nadia, the mother of the little patient I am going to discuss, receive only prescriptions, medical diagnoses, and test results.

The mother's story

In Nadia's case, when the doctors did not manage to control her anxiety or her infant's excessive crying with medication, they lost interest in the case. They blamed Nadia's anxiety for the situation and prescribed anti-anxiety drugs. No one inquired into her personal history to make sense of what she was feeling.

Here is the story Nadia told me at our first interview. She and her husband had moved from Russia just after the death of her maternal grandmother, whom she adored. On her arrival in the United States, Nadia found herself in an unknown place, alone, pregnant, grieving for the loss of her grandmother, having to cope with adjusting to a totally new lifestyle. In addition, she had to adjust to becoming a mother without any previous experience of infants, for she had always worked as a financial consultant. Her husband was constantly traveling to faraway places for his job, and her mother and other family were far away. She felt lonely and uncontained but denied all her negative feelings, only allowing herself to "feel good" and try harder: the perfect situation for feelings of abandonment, deprivation, and loss to set in. Nadia relegated her negative feelings to the unconscious and this constellated a negative mother archetypal field.

The infant was born prematurely by Caesarean section and cried inconsolably for the first three months of her life, refusing to feed from the breast. The doctors not only failed to support the new mother, but she also felt that they blamed her for becoming too anxious.

The archetype of the hero

As I have described in my paper about Oedipus, when an attempt is made to deny personal limitations and the vulnerability derived from feelings of abandonment, the hero archetype, along with a negative parental couple, becomes constellated in the unconscious (Sidoli 1995: 49). In that paper I described how, given the circumstances of his early abandonment, Oedipus had to become a hero in order to survive. The hero archetype is usually constellated in difficult situations in life, because imagining being able to overcome extreme difficulties offers a temporary illusion of triumph over feelings of helplessness and impotence. By accomplishing great deeds, a hero avoids feeling helpless, that is to say, he adopts a manic defense against his depressed feelings.

As for Nadia, identification with the hero had been her habitual mode of dealing with distressing situations in her life, because since childhood she could not expect to receive psychological support from the adults in her family circle. In Jung's view, the hero is constellated to counteract the insignificance represented by the child archetype. He writes, "[T]he hero's nature is human but raised to the limit of the supernatural – he is 'semi-divine' . . . The motifs of 'insignificance,' exposure, abandonment, danger, etc. try to show how precarious is the psychic possibility of wholeness" (Jung 1951a: 166).

Since no one in her new environment seemed to pay attention to her hidden distress, Nadia denied and hid her distress even more. This naturally led her to cut the connection with the feelings of her own inner child and consequently prevented her from empathizing with her newborn's vulnerability and distress; she could not calm her baby's inconsolable cry.

After a difficult delivery, and far away from her mother, Nadia was confronted with situations in which she felt vulnerable and helpless. Rather than break down, her traumatized ego adopted the heroic defense. Her negative emotions, denied access to and rejected from consciousness, were relegated to her split-off shadow, the bad infant, and projected onto the "bad doctors" (cf. Sidoli 1995).

The baby

Following a difficult birth experience, the newborn Marsha landed in the lap of a mother whose psyche offered her no inner space where she could process and make sense of her affects and distressed states. Thus in the absence of the appropriate "maternal reverie," the infant self, too, adopted a heroic withdrawal within itself in order to survive. Michael Fordham has called such survival strategy in infancy a "defense of the self" (Fordham 1976). It can be understood as an autistic withdrawal. Frances Tustin also described these autistic defenses in infancy. In her work with autistic children she defined two types of autistic defense: encapsulation and enmeshment. In her book *The Protective Shell in Children and Adults*, Tustin writes:

> I see pathological autism as a warped exaggeration of a psycho-chemical, neuro-mental reaction that is an innate protective measure against the trauma of bodily hurt, either illusory or actual. It is a rigid overdevelopment of the normal processes of shutting out of one's mind those affairs that cannot be handled at the moment.
>
> (Tustin 1990: 43)

Autistic children are different from any other children that we see. Most of the younger children are mute; older ones may be echolalic. The most outstanding characteristic, which differentiates them from any other type of patients, is that they are averted from relationship with people . . . . They seem to be surrounded by a shell which prevents us from getting in touch with them. The reasons for this are different in each case, but my own work indicates that it is often an interaction between a mothering person who, through no fault of her own, could not be as in touch with the baby as she would have liked to be, and a particularly sensitive baby who tended to shy away from a degree of frustration that a more placid baby would have been able to tolerate. Also in many cases the influence of the father had not been sufficiently felt as a source of strength for both mother and baby.

(Tustin 1990: 35–6)

In my view, Tustin's theory explains the arrest in emotional development in the case of my little patient. Marsha's instinctual expectations and developmental rhythms appeared hampered and disturbed by her mother's depressed state, for which Nadia had received no understanding or support. For her part, Nadia was unable to make sense of or process her infant's difficulties at birth and after birth. In this situation the infant was left in the grip of her primitive anxieties. We can imagine that she had experienced birth as a catastrophic falling apart, and resorted to autistic defensive behavior. The father's frequent absences exacerbated the situation for both mother and infant.

From puppet to child

Three-year-old Marsha was brought to me by her mother with a diagnosis of autism. According to Nadia the pediatrician had felt unable to help Marsha, had become angry with her for her violent tantrums and difficult behavior in his office, and had referred her for psychological assessment.

During the course of three months I saw Marsha with her mother for 24 sessions of parent–infant psychotherapy. I decided on this type of intervention because Marsha did not speak a word of English and her mother appeared to need a lot of help to make sense of her child's babbling. The family came from Russia and, according to Nadia, Marsha's language was a muddled mixture of nursery rhymes and chanting of stories in Russian on tapes that she liked to listen to.

Nadia had telephoned me in great distress, asking me to see her child while expressing doubts that I might be able to help her because, she said, the child did not relate to anybody. She did not know what to do because the family was supposed to return to their home country and she felt ashamed of her child's state. Marsha lived in a world of her own and she was afraid that her child might be beyond help because she had been seen by many doctors here and in her own country and nobody had been able to help. All this was communicated in a rapid, anxious way during the course of the first phone call as if Nadia could not contain it a minute longer. I reassured her that I would like to see the child and that if the problem had emotional roots I might be able to help her, but of course I could give her no guarantees. So she agreed to come and bring Marsha to meet me.

The first session

Thus the following week at the time of the session I opened the door and a pretty, petite brunette woman appeared. A beautiful, blonde, frail little girl was trailing floppily behind her. The mother seemed extremely anxious and could not stop talking, wanting to fill me in on her difficulties with Marsha. She presented me with a two-page typed list of all her and her husband's concerns about the child's developmental delays as if reporting from a manual of child development.

While her mother talked, Marsha wandered about in a self-absorbed way as if the two of us did not exist. She walked on her tiptoes and looked uninterested. She seemed to be in another world and for many sessions she did not make eye contact with me or her mother or look at the objects in the room. She did not seek physical contact with her mother, nor did her mother attempt to touch or hug her. I kept watching her, trying to find an opportunity to engage her, but she gave me no clues. Meanwhile her mother started reading me the list of her concerns.

I kept watching Marsha. She moved around the room in a detached way and yet, as her mother's anxiety and distress grew while reading her list of concerns, I began to experience some apprehension and fear in Marsha. When I became sure of the child's fear, I asked Nadia to translate to Marsha all that I was going to say. Nadia politely agreed but added that she did not want me to be disappointed because she knew that Marsha would not understand or respond. Then she added sheepishly that she believed Marsha might be retarded. I replied gently but firmly that now it was my turn to decide what was the problem with Marsha, and her role was to be an interpreter. She agreed to do this but did not

look very convinced. I began to talk to Marsha via her mother's trans-
lation, telling her that I believed she was very afraid that I might hurt her
because she did not know who I was.

I decided that, since the mother believed that the child would not
respond, I would take the opposite approach and assume that she did
understand and would eventually signal some sort of response. Thus I
put into words every gesture that Marsha made, running a constant
commentary on her behavior.

I offered her a box full of toys, but she did not even bother to look at
them. Nadia kept running a negative commentary, warning me each time
that Marsha failed to respond, that she never responded and did not
understand anyway. I believe that she was projecting into me her sense
of hopelessness and frustration about her child to make me feel as hopeless as she herself felt.

Although I did not really know what was going to happen, I reassured
her, insisting that I knew what I was doing. I pointed out that she was
puzzled by my approach to her child, one that no other professional had
taken before. I explained that my approach was based on psychoanalytic
understanding and that I believed that inside Marsha was a part of her
that had withdrawn because she was terrified, and that I was trying to
engage that part to draw her out of her state of fear. I said that Marsha
would need to trust me enough to let go of some of her present behavior
that I thought constituted a primitive defense against an early terror and
survival panic.

I noticed Nadia's puzzlement and considered this a positive sign. I
shifted to comment on her own feelings of fear, disappointment, and
hopelessness about Marsha. She began to talk about her expectations
and how Marsha had never been normal from the moment she was born.
Marsha by now had kicked the toy box and was climbing on the couch
and tumbling down on to the floor with a flip. Her body movements
became more coordinated and began to show a sense of purpose. Marsha
seemed to respond to our talking by using body movements instead of
language, the way that a young infant does by kicking rhythmically at
the sound of mother's voice. To me it seemed like an echoing by the
child of the mother's release of feelings that had never before been put
into words. But it was also a beginning of letting go in both mother and
child. So I asked Nadia to tell me about Marsha's birth and her feelings
about what had happened then, wondering if something had gone wrong
during the birth process given that she had said the child was born
"difficult." I agreed with her that Marsha was a difficult child indeed,
but I also told her that premature newborns have extreme difficulties

adapting to the dramatic change from intrauterine life to life outside the womb and that maybe Marsha had been such an infant.

For the first time I felt I had given Nadia something she could hang on to and feel less anxious and guilty about. It was clear that she had unconsciously blamed herself for Marsha's problems. She immediately told me that Marsha was born by Caesarean section and that although she was full-term she had water in her lungs like a premature baby and had trouble breathing and sucking from the very start. She complained that the hospital had discharged her after one day and that she had to struggle with the baby at home on her own. She then added that in her own country it is different. A health visitor and a midwife come regularly for the first months to help and support the mother. Here she had felt lost, completely on her own with this crying baby, and she despaired of being able to help her.

Her words offered me the first opening to comment on how displaced she must have felt and homesick for her mother and her own country at that time. Although she quickly denied this, I felt that communication had begun to open up between us. In this way the first interview ended. We decided that she would come with the child twice weekly during the time before their departure, which she anticipated in about three months.

I told her that, given the limited time, I would see what I could do but could not guarantee what would happen. However, I had hopes because the child did not seem to me to be autistic; rather I thought that she was using powerful autistic defenses out of fear of letting people come close. Marsha followed like a toy on wheels being passively pulled by her mother, without acknowledging my goodbye.

I knew that the first contact with the mother had been positive and hoped that this would allow the child eventually to trust me. I speculated that Nadia might have communicated to Marsha a mistrust for people who were not her own people, a mistrust that I could now see she felt herself. In fact, she only allowed the child to be looked after by a nanny from her own country who did not speak English and to socialize with compatriots of her parents. It seemed to me that the mother had not really settled in the foreign environment, which felt alien to her, but that she had denied this.

In my countertransference from the very start I felt instant attachment and deep warmth for Marsha whom I found attractive and mysterious. This often happens with such autistic children, and I felt connected to her in some deep ways. Although I felt a certain amount of annoyance and irritation with the mother for her totally non-psychological way of thinking, at the same time I could empathize with her distress and loneliness. Perhaps because I too had my first baby when living abroad it was easier to tune in to her difficulties. The fact that I was from Italy was also a factor that allowed the mother to bond with me, for according to her, Russians and Italians are alike.

Archetypal emotions at the time of birth

As I described more fully in the previous chapter, birth is an archetypal event that has an impact on the environment in which it occurs because it brings about permanent changes. In turn, the event of birth is dramatically influenced by that same environment. It has major psychological implications because it cathects an unconscious archetypal representation in the psyche, the archetype of beginning, which gives rise to a multitude of images related to change and beginnings. The psyche uses these images in an attempt to depict its own origins, and the way we come into the world has great implications for the way we are going to live and deal with other beginnings in life.

Nadia seemed to have been negatively affected by the highly technical procedures used in maternity hospitals and the cold, functional atmosphere of birth where hardly any room is provided for the parents' emotions, or for the baby who will be created and shaped by their imagination. This lack of empathic attunement, I believe, must also correspond to some of Nadia's own early experience of attachment to a cold mother who was not attuned to her needs. She must also have been influenced by the loss of her grandmother at the time of her departure from Russia, which left her "motherless." The minimal time that Nadia was allowed to recover in the hospital after a Caesarean delivery was experienced by her as callous and made her feel uncared-for. Hence she was emotionally unable to care for her baby, to whom she offered the same kind of mechanical care that she had received. For his part, the father was not allowed to take time off work to be with her, and no one from the hospital visited the home to follow up the mother–baby relationship to support mother and infant in dealing with difficulties in the early attachment stage.

It is clear from Nadia's complaints to me that she had been unable to complain to the doctors or the hospital about the kind of care she had received. Instead she had felt extremely deprived, idealizing her culture of origin, where, she stated, the birth event was celebrated with greater mythological and traditional collective rituals, which she had missed. It is clear that she had felt homesick, but I also had to wonder what had prevented her from demanding the support she deserved, unless there was in her an internal mother who would not listen to her complaints.

Thus, Nadia's inner space at the time of Marsha's birth was contaminated with unconscious primitive emotional elements, both from her relationship with her mother and also from the cold, insensitive medical culture which affected the mother–infant relationship negatively, in spite of the extremely attentive physical care and concern that this mother devoted to her infant.

In Jungian terms, we can say that an archetypal field is like a bath where the water may be polluted by maternal/parental frustrations and disappointed expectations about the developing infant, as well as by cultural approaches to birth and delivery. Unconscious parental expectations may range from inflated expectations of the Messiah/Savior to ominous fears, as in the case of Oedipus. I believe that Nadia had become deeply discouraged and slowly had given up hope for her child's positive development, becoming resigned to Marsha's "mental retardation." It was the sense of shame about returning home that prompted Nadia to give Marsha's potential a last chance. Fortunately, I struck up a positive relationship with Nadia and managed to get in touch with Marsha from the start, even though it was on a very primitive level.

The second session

When they came back for the second session Marsha looked slightly more present. She seemed to recognize the place and for the first time requested that all lights in the room should be lit. This ritual had to be performed at the beginning of every session from that day on or she would throw a tantrum and would try to turn on the lights herself in a very insistent way. I thought this might be related to her wish to establish better eye contact but did not comment about it.

Marsha noticed the toy box and her attention was drawn to two little plastic teacups with saucers and two little spoons. She got them out, put them on a side table and started mumbling some words to herself and humming a tune. Her mother promptly told me that these words did not make any sense. She said that Marsha seemed to have mixed them up with a song from a videotape story in which the protagonist pours out water for his horses to drink and sings a tune similar to the one she was mumbling. At this point Marsha signaled to Nadia that she wanted water. Mother had not noticed, so I said out loud: "Now Marsha is asking you for water." I thought that Marsha's difficulties might also be due to the way in which mother was misattuned to her nonverbal signals.

Thinking that the request for water could refer to Marsha's early suck-ing struggles and to having had water in her lungs, I commented that now Marsha wanted to have Mara's water because it was like good mommy's milk. I gave her the water in a little jug and she spent the remaining part of the session pouring the water from one cup to the other, then putting it back into the jug while chanting her mysterious words in a monotonous way. Whenever the water spilled on the floor she appeared anxious and gestured to her mother for paper to mop it up. I commented about her fear that the cups were peeing on my floor and messing it all up and that I might get angry with her.

While all this was going on Nadia was trying to convince me that Marsha's activity did not make any sense. I agreed with Nadia that at first sight Marsha's behavior was very puzzling. But I believed that it was a communication of something which had been impressed on Marsha's mind and which she as yet had no words to communicate, but that I was working at understanding the puzzle.

Towards the end of the session Marsha began to run around the room humming her tune, looking completely cut off from us and lost, as if in a strange other place. I noticed however that she was interested in my big green swinging chair and had tentatively tried to sit in it. I promptly commented on that and encouraged her to sit on my chair, pushing it up and down like a swing. I said that Marsha wanted to sit on my chair like on my lap. She seemed to like that and made some excited sounds, but returned very quickly to her water-mixing activity in an anxious way. At the end of the session she went away without acknowledging my goodbye.

Ongoing therapy

The next session continued more or less unchanged with Marsha obses-sively repeating the water game and my commenting on her wanting water from me because my water was good for the horses and for baby Marsha inside her. She alternated the water game with running to my chair and doing gymnastics.

In the third session she finally tasted and drank the water herself. She drank from each cup and afterwards ordered me to refill them. I commented that now my water was good for Marsha to drink and that it made her feel good inside. This game also continued unchanged with Marsha drinking increasing amounts of water, much to her mother's surprise, as she said that Marsha never drank water. Meanwhile, I punctuated my comments with a series of high-pitched sounds and exaggerated facial expressions the way that mothers do when "talking" to their young infant.

Nadia kept translating obediently but appeared increasingly bewildered by my strange "unscientific" approach. The more Marsha drank water the more her body appeared to be free to move and to jump all over the room, to roll on the floor and exhibit her acrobatic abilities, which I praised. I said that Marsha wanted to dance and could be like a ballerina in my room because she liked it and she felt good in here as she did with her daddy. Her mother had told me that the acrobatic activity was what Marsha and her father always did together. This indicated to me that Marsha had a more physical relationship with her father and enjoyed using his body to support her, whereas at the start of the treatment she did not approach her mother's body for comfort. Apparently Marsha liked to sit on her father's shoulders and be carried about by him, on the top of the world. She would then exhibit her agility in a series of complex pirouettes and eventually would dive down to the floor, climb back up and start the exercises all over again while exhibiting great delight and excitement. She showed an extremely well developed sense of balance and physical coordination, while her hand movements looked frozen by comparison. She soon started wanting to climb on my shoulders too and to jump on my back from the top of my chair.

I commented that she enjoyed climbing on my back, as she did when Daddy was home to play with her. She made a lot of excited sounds and laughed, making funny faces. She increasingly made eye contact with me; at first she quickly looked away but then became more able to sustain the look and to smile at me.

Her behavior was structured in the following ritualistic way: she would come in, rush to the toy box, reach frantically for the cups, demand imperiously to have them filled, chant her tune while filling and emptying the cups, drink the water, accompanying the drinking with gestures of delight that she was imitating from me. Then she would stop this game suddenly, rush to my green chair, demanding to be rocked and pushed on it, climbing all the way to the top of the back of the chair, as though on her father's shoulders, pirouetting up there, balancing herself and using my body to hold her steady. She would then throw herself down the back of the chair while I would make exaggerated frightened dramatic sounds of, "Ups, patapumfete, down Marsha falls!" She responded by making happy sounds while at the same time demanding that I hold her tightly by the ankles to keep her from falling off the chair onto the floor. All her demands were communicated with imperious gestures, and she immediately became frustrated if I did not understand. I continued my step-by-step commentary for several sessions and no new features evolved. The most important thing for Marsha was to be able to repeat her activities endlessly and she became very frustrated if I tried to change them.

Her mother commented on the obsessive quality of her play and I agreed with her, but also added that infants normally learn from repetitions and hate changes. In the meantime Nadia was talking more freely about her own difficulties in adapting to the many changes continually occurring in her life. She mentioned problems in her relationship with her husband, his obsessional traits, and the stubbornness that runs in her husband's family which she could recognize also in Marsha. So, I commented, we knew where Marsha's obsessional behavior came from! By making this link, Marsha was no longer a strange, alien being in her mother's mind but was acquiring human characteristics typical of her father's family.

This conversation led Nadia to talk about her husband, his disappointment and worry because of Marsha's arrest in development, and his concern for her mental abilities. Nadia then complained that Marsha, who seemed so happy to play active excited games with her father, did not look for him or ask where he was each time he left for his long business trips. However, she looked happy to see him when he returned. I asked Nadia how she felt about his trips herself, and she finally admitted that it was not easy to be left alone with Marsha and her disturbed behavior. At times she felt she was going crazy too. Then she rationalized that he had to travel for his job. I then said that maybe both she and Marsha tried to forget about his leaving, in order not to feel too distressed and abandoned.

Again I felt I had touched a sore spot in Nadia. I amplified her need to be supported and added that perhaps both she and Marsha felt more secure when daddy was around to protect them in a foreign place. Nadia opened up more and talked about her life back home, and her mother-in-law who had been a teacher of special education, one of the best in her country, who had received national recognition for her abilities. She added that when they went back, surely her mother-in-law would want to fix Marsha. Nadia was worried because she felt the mother-in-law was too rigid about discipline. She feared Marsha would hate it and throw a fit as she usually did when forced to do what she did not want to do. There was no mention of Nadia's own mother except that, because of the shortage of homes, when she returned to Russia she would have to stay at her mother's place and her husband would have to stay with his mother until they found a family home. I commented that this might cause stress, but she denied it.

Then Nadia told me that Marsha refused to be toilet-trained, which embarrassed and worried her a lot. Marsha did not seem to care, she said. I suggested that maybe she was being too rigid about it, maybe imposing rules on the child as her mother or mother-in-law might have done. Nadia burst out crying and complained that she herself could not tolerate the child messing herself at her age. To avoid this, she was carrying a potty in a plastic bag whenever they went out, and she would make Marsha sit on it at regular intervals. I suggested that Marsha was resisting the toilet-training in opposition to her mother, in an attempt to assert herself at the cost of holding onto her bodily contents even if this was painful. I suggested she try to ignore the issue for a while in order to diffuse it.

All this time Marsha was repeating her games, apparently not paying attention to what her mother and I were saying, and yet I could observe bodily changes in her as reactions to her mother's emotional states.

Nadia appeared to have listened to my suggestion about toilet-training because the potty disappeared. The following session she brought up Marsha's eating difficulties, complaining that she had always been difficult: even as an infant she would not take the breast.

Marsha kept playing with the water, jumping on my chair, and running around the room, but engaging me more and more in a physical way with sounds and mime. She was fighting with her mother for my attention. I felt like a mother of twins having to split myself between the two to contain both of them within the field of my attention.

Marsha had now added a new element to her games. After the water game, she jumped onto my chair and did all her gymnastics, but now she said that she was tired and lay down on the couch close to her mother. I said that now Marsha was tired and wanted to go to sleep close to mommy. She liked this idea very much, and a new stage in her play developed. Nadia told me that she had difficulty in getting Marsha to sleep and that in the night she often woke up with nightmares.

Here I would like to illustrate the syntonic alternating of mother and child in presenting material for me to work on. In response to Nadia's communication, Marsha lay down, resting her head on her mother's lap for the first time, then wriggled down from the couch, collected all the soft cushions in the room, piled them on top of herself and sang a tune which told the story of a crocodile. I commented that Marsha could not go to sleep because she was afraid that a bad crocodile would come and eat her up. Marsha kept wriggling and hiding under the cushions. The mother protested and explained to me that the crocodile in Marsha's song was a jolly, happy one. Again I had to tell her to translate what I was saying even if she did not agree with me and eventually she did. I kept telling Marsha about the horrible crocodile that wanted to eat her up. Marsha asked that I hide behind my chair and another ritual developed. She had to go under the pillows and I had to wish her goodnight. She had to wish me goodnight. I had to say that she could sleep safely because her mother would send the crocodile away and I had to pretend to go to sleep too and snore. (I suppose I had to be father.)

After having slept long enough she would jump out from among her pillows, say it was morning and, all cheerful, shout good morning to me to wake me up. The game had to be repeated again and again until she felt ready to get up, run back to the water game and drink from the cups, even offering drinks to her mother and me.

I was interested to notice the progress in Marsha's behavior, which was becoming related to me and to her mother in a different way. Her mother noticed the changes too and was happy about them but could not understand what I had done to make them come about. She asked me if there was something she could read in order to carry on with what I was doing with Marsha once they returned home. I suggested that she should pay attention to Marsha as I was doing, and, most of all, always talk to her if she wanted the child to develop language. At this point she revealed that in fact Marsha's language had definitely improved. Now she was trying to form sentences even though she did not use the pronoun "I" and used verbs in the infinitive. By this time I had seen her more than ten sessions and I had become more hopeful of being able to stabilize the changes that were occurring in Marsha.

I gave Nadia the names of a few books but, more important, I told her that I would provide her with the name of a child psychotherapist who could continue to work with Marsha once they returned home, because, whatever result we would achieve, she needed to be followed up for progress to continue. Nadia agreed, but I could sense that she was beginning to grieve the prospect of leaving me.

Further developments occurred the following session when I introduced some Lego bricks. Marsha took to this toy and began to build complicated tower-like buildings with great concentration. She would make sure that both her mother and I watched her and she wanted to be praised when she finished. Then she broke down her buildings into a heap of pieces and ran to my chair, played at falling down, and eventually rushed to sit on the heap of Lego bricks and say, "A heap of pieces fallen down."

At first I was puzzled by this behavior, but then I suggested that Marsha felt as if she were falling apart. This seemed to make sense to her, for she started to repeat this game with ritualistic precision as she had done with the other games. I imagined that she was enacting the experience of an infant feeling uncontained by her mother's mind, experiencing falling apart and going to pieces, which seemed likely, given the fact that Nadia had felt so distressed at the time of Marsha's birth.

By the tenth session Marsha was able to relate to me, greeted me, and was happy to come to see me, and became upset each time she had to leave. In this way she demonstrated her increasing capacity to form attachments. I kept telling her that we would stop seeing each other soon because she and her parents had to go back home. She did not seem to hear it until about the nineteenth session, when she threw a terrible tantrum when it was time to leave. It took great exertion by her mother and me to hold her down and calm her because she used enormous strength and fought us as if to save her life. I managed to get her out of the door, but she squeezed herself between the door and doorframe and screamed in despair while trying to push her way back into the room. I tried to close the door, telling her it was time for her to go home, but to no avail. This drama lasted for a good fifteen minutes beyond the end of the session. She sounded desperate and it was hard to tolerate her screaming and her protests. I felt horrible having to push her out. Finally she let her mother drag her away while Nadia too was crying in distress. I believe Marsha was expressing her despair, frustration, and helplessness at the impending separation. After this violent protest she did not show any further distress, and at our last session she said goodbye and walked out without turning back to give me a last look, as she had been accustomed to do.

Her father came to the last session to thank me. He was pleased with his daughter's improvement and took many photographs of the child and me in the room. He gave me a photograph of Marsha for me to remember her by. I felt very moved by his gesture and by the way he was able to express his good feelings. He was more effusive than the mother, who also expressed many warm feelings and sadness for the ending.

They left and I felt an enormous sense of loss and sadness, hoping for weeks that I would hear from them, as Nadia had promised she would call me to let me know how Marsha was doing. But I did not hear anything for four months. Then a friend of the family who had visited them in their new residence brought me a message that Marsha was doing well and that they remembered me, sent their greetings and would be in touch again soon. Every now and then I looked at Marsha's picture and wished her and her parents well, because I felt that the work had been proceeding well and felt very frustrated by the premature ending. I was sure that with an open-ended analytic therapy she would have had a better prognosis.

Discussion

I believe that at birth Marsha experienced *disintegration* of the primary self, and not *deintegration* as described by Fordham, for she exhibited autistic features. I suggest that the disintegrative experience was produced by her respiratory difficulties and the other emotional circumstances of her birth, which must have aroused dread and panic in the self. The panic may have induced choking fears any time she attempted to breathe or to feed at the breast. From this dreadful experience, defenses of the self had become activated in her which had made her feel safe by reverting to an intrauterine experience of containment. In this way the normal rhythms of the deintegration–reintegration process of the primary self (Fordham) could not be properly activated at birth and parts of her remained in limbo until, in the course of the therapy, I was able to process for her in my mind the early catastrophic experiences that had blocked her development. In Bion's terms, I was able to perform the reverie that her mother had not been able to manage for the reasons described above, transforming unformed unthinkable elements by using my mind to think about them (beta into alpha). Adopting Jungian concepts, I could say that I reached out into the psychoid area where Marsha and her mother were imprisoned in a field of archetypal fantasies of monstrous mothers and infants, and helped them begin to transform these into human-like experiences. In this way the archetypal, primitive elements were rinsed out of the contaminated bathwater, and the baby, who risked being thrown away with the dirty water, could be fished out, comforted, and helped to let go of some of the primitive terror that had gripped her.

An element that struck me in the therapy was the syntony between the mother's and the child's processes, and how, as the mother reached an insight, the child would exhibit more related behavior. Therefore I believe that my decision to see the two of them in mother–infant therapy was the right therapeutic approach to break down their negative, symbiotic enmeshment, and to create a space in the mother's mind that could process her own feelings and consequently those of her child. My positive and warm countertransference to both of them was an important factor that offered them the needed maternal container that had been missing. Feeling supported, Nadia began to relate to her daughter in a new way. She became curious about Marsha and her feelings and tried to decode her nonverbal communications, imitating my approach in a positive identification with me. I felt that both of them experienced me as a mother who accepted that they felt lost and frightened and helped them make sense of their feelings in a way that was new. It helped Nadia to understand her child's communications and needs, make sense of them, and accept her as different from herself. In this way Marsha was allowed to begin to develop language as a way of reaching out to her mother in a symbolic way and begin to come out of the defensive autistic shell in which she had been encapsulated.

Postscript

Some months after writing this chapter I received a long letter from Nadia in which she described the difficulties Marsha had in leaving her familiar home to go to live with her grandmother in Russia. She gave an account of the three medical/psychological interventions that they experienced on Marsha's account, and while child psychotherapy is not available, they receive support from a psychologist whom they trust. Marsha has grown two inches, although she is still small for her age, and sometimes Nadia cannot resist passing her off as only three years old, although she is a year and a half older. She does not relate well to other children but does play active games with them. She enjoys dressing up to visit friends, and uses language to describe events in her life, such as a visit to the zoo, in a kind of telegraphic prose. When she acts out a story, she dresses the part and acts beautifully, like a normal child.

Many of her stereotypic movements and habits have gone, she is more easy-going, talks better, and eats a more varied diet. But her mother was worried about how she would get on in a pre-school class where children are interested in relating to each other in both positive and negative ways.

Chapter 3

The Jungian infant

Is there a valid theoretical construct to describe an infant from a Jungian perspective? I have been attempting to answer this question since 1982 when I started teaching infant observation seminars at the Society of Analytical Psychology in London. These seminars became an integral part of the Child Analytic Training Program.

We have been familiar for some time with the Kleinian infant, who lives in a world of unconscious fantasies, and with the Winnicottian infant, who is enveloped by the maternal preoccupation. But the Jungian infant, who lives in an archetypal world, is a fairly new construct since Jungians traditionally have not been very interested in infancy as a fundamental part of life. Michael Fordham was the first Jungian to show interest in infancy and to apply Jung's theory to this stage of life.

Following Fordham's theory, I hypothesized that, given the fact that an infant's experience is primarily affective, it therefore resides in the psychosomatic realm of the self. In infancy, archetypal activity in the self is very much related to instinctual drives and the discharge of intense emotions.

The seminars in infant observation, in which flesh-and-blood infants are closely observed in their daily relationship with their mothers, confirmed my hypothesis.

In developing a theoretical construct to underpin these infant observation courses, I took into account Jung's theories, which he developed from the analyses of his adult patients, together with Fordham's theories on infancy. These theories fit the extreme affective level of the infant experience we observed. This construct is neither antithetical to nor irreconcilable with other conceptual frames, such as Klein's.

The Jungian developmental frame

This Jungian conceptual frame made it possible to introduce infant observation to the Jungian world. Fordham understood that Jung's theory of the psyche needed to be applicable to the onset of life and to childhood. When I started teaching infant observation seminars, I felt that infant observation could provide the means to demonstrate and confirm the validity of Fordham's brilliant intuition.

My hypothesis was that concepts such as the self and the primary self (Fordham's definition of the self at the onset of life) ought to be observable in an infant's behavior. I further hypothesized that Jung's concept of the archetypes and Fordham's descriptions of deintegrative and reintegrative sequences by which the self and the ego develop would also be observable in infancy.

I will now briefly outline the essential aspects of Jung's thinking that Fordham applied to infancy.

Jung's theory of the psyche

Jung conceived of the self as the totality of the psyche, combining the conscious with the unconscious and containing the ego and the archetypes. However, he also paradoxically viewed the self as the archetype of order. Jung conceived the archetypes as the organizers of experience, which operate within the self in the service of the ego. These are innate predispositions which, although not characterized by the quality of experience which we call consciousness, nonetheless determine and structure the relationship between the internal and external world. Therefore, the archetype in itself is not knowable, but is manifested endopsychically and gives rise to typical imagery, which has archetypal characteristics. All archetypes have a positive and a negative side – a life-enhancing and a life-destroying potential. Jung implied that the archetypes contain *in potentia* the ontological genesis of the human race.

Fordham developed the concept of the "primary self" from Jung's concept of the self. In Fordham's view the primary self represents the totality of the psyche and soma in a germinal state. He conceptualized the primary self as a blueprint, a steady state of integration from which the child's ego and bodily growth will unfold through a dynamic process that he termed deintegration–reintegration.

Jung defined archetypes as the mental representations of instinctual drives and/or the innate predisposition to experience life according to certain patterns, as well as a powerful way of representing affects. In

Jung's view affects are the lifeblood of the psyche. Perhaps even more significantly, affects are the bridge between body and psyche, instinct and spirit, whereby they influence the psychosoma.

Fordham assumed that archetypes were activated at the onset of life, from within the womb, and that an infant from conception on is an individual in its own right, contained in the womb but separate from the mother.

Fordham conceived of the archetypes as dynamic structures closely related to drives, expressed in impulses originating in neurophysiological structures and biochemical changes. He writes:

> [T]he theory of archetypes could be seen to bring body and psyche together. Jung's thesis as to their bipolarity then became particularly meaningful: the archetypes can be conceived as unconscious entities having two poles, the one expressing itself in instinctual impulses and drives, the other in the form of fantasies. In contrast to the instinctual drives, which are relatively fixed and few in number, the fantasy (or spiritual) component has wide and flexible application.
>
> (Fordham 1976: 6)

In early infancy neurophysiological drives and discharges prevail. Hence the quality of the infant's experience is totally archetypal, that is to say, it is ruled by affects and emotions in response to being bombarded by undifferentiated stimuli that tend to overwhelm the developing ego consciousness.

About emotion Jung wrote:

> Emotion is the alchemical fire whose warmth brings everything into existence and whose heat burns all superfluities to ashes . . . . But on the other hand emotion is the moment when steel meets flint and a spark is struck forth, for emotion is the chief source of consciousness. There is no change from darkness to light or from inertia to movement without emotion.
>
> (Jung 1938: 96)

Infantile experiences, which are loaded with emotions and affects, are the source of all numinous archetypal imagery which surfaces in fantasies and dreams in later life.

At the fetal stage and in early infancy, ego function is rudimentary. Therefore, we can only infer the existence of proto-images, such as shapes and patterns which, enriched by sensory experiences and memory traces, will in time develop into mental representations of self and other. In infancy instinctual needs have an overwhelming urgency, which is expressed by the infant through fits of screaming, panic, and other affect-loaded somatizations.

The psychic energy bound up in the primary self divides into opposites, constellating the opposing archetypal experiences, psycho-physiological in nature. There is an opening up of the self (deintegration) during which positive and negative experiences take place.

Positive experiences lead to good, satisfactory, loving, and comforting feelings in the infant, which Jungians attribute to the good mother archetype (good breast, good holding, good loving mother, and good loving infant).

When negative experiences occur, leading to feelings of discomfort, hate, despair, rage, violence, persecution, fear, and panic, the infant experiences both itself and its mother as destroyed by the baby's own violent impulses, and the negative mother archetype is constellated (bad breast and unspeakable dread).

The deintegrative phase is followed by a digestive phase called re-integration. This is a phase in which the self closes up again to digest the newly acquired experiences in order to integrate them. The new experiences coalesce around pre-existing intrauterine proto-experiences and contribute to ego growth.

Both the "loving creative" and the "violent destructive" experiences have a quality of absoluteness. They are absolute for the infant; nothing else exists but that particular experience in which he or she is completely involved. Jung stresses absoluteness as an attribute of the self, indicating that in the infant the self is active and predominates over the ego.

In its postnatal phase the ego is fragmentary and, to use Jung's imagery, is emerging like many small islands in the vast sea of the unconscious.

The mother is of the utmost importance in this phase. Her psychological task is to intervene and support with her adult ego her infant's ego in the same way that she looks after the baby's physical needs. Thus she transforms into thoughts and ideas and gives a name to the affective experiences that the baby is living through.

The energy released in the deintegrative phase produces instability and tension, which drive the infant towards the outer world (breast/mother) in an attempt to re-establish the original stable state (*homeostasis*).

Here it is important to underline a major difference between

Fordham's and Klein's conceptualization of the ego in infancy. For Klein the ego is present at birth and functions in relation to the primitive survival anxiety generated by the death instinct. For Fordham the ego is very rudimentary at birth and is born out of the dynamism of the primary self through the archetypal process of deintegration–reintegration, which is a normal developmental process related to the survival of all natural beings.

From experiences caused by the alternation of deintegrative/reintegrative sequences over a period of several months, the infant grows in his body and develops an inner world.

The emergence of consciousness and ego-structuring takes place within the nursing couple's activities, supported by maternal care. In the course of deintegrative/reintegrative sequences the infant introjects experiences and assimilates them emotionally, physically, and mentally. In the first two years of life the infant experiences both the terrifying and the life-giving omnipotent aspects of the mother archetype, which he will project onto the real mother, who is more comforting and, above all, infinitely less powerful than the archetype. In this way the infant can come to terms with both his own and his mother's limitations. He accepts his own limited areas of competence as compensatory, rather than relying on a fantasized, unrealistic omnipotence.

Initially the maternal interventions have to be immediate. Gradually, however, the integration process begins and seems to occur in the following manner. With the strengthening of the ego, the infant manages to remember the experience of maternal care (good breast) for increasingly long spans of time and to invoke it in times of need or distress during deintegrative phases. As time goes by, the infant's ego becomes strong enough to substitute in place of the real mother the introjected maternal function, so that he can bear frustrations, difficulties, anxieties, and waiting with greater ease.

The experience of an internalized good-enough breast takes place when the successful feedings and loving care the infant receives outnumber his negative experiences of deprivation, frustration, and bad fits with the breast, and also when the mother has realistic expectations of herself and her infant.

In this way the experience of reality begins to differentiate itself from the archetypal image. In non-pathological situations, the archetypal experience recedes as the archetypal images become incarnated in human experiences. When bad experiences outnumber the good ones, or when the mother is unable to frustrate the infant enough to give him a sense of realistic limitations, the relationship remains omnipotent and in the archetypal realm. In that case the archetypal images continue to predominate and to be projected by the infant onto the mother and by the mother onto the infant.

Paul

In this example, we witness a situation where a mother responds quickly to the urgency of the instinctual hunger discharge of her infant so peace can be quickly restored. However, because of powerful deintegrative sequences due to the infant Paul's vigorous instinctual needs, the situation deteriorates over time. Paul is the third child in the family, and the mother cannot always respond promptly to the urgency of his demands. The other children and her husband also have claims on her time. She begins to feel overwhelmed; her own chaotic internal feelings get activated in response to Paul's fits and frustration. She begins to feel she is a "bad mother" and to experience Paul as a "bad baby." In this way the stage is set for a cycle of negative interactions dominated by anxiety, frustration, and persecution in both mother and infant. An observation recorded when Paul was twelve days old shows the beginning of the deterioration in the relationship.

The doorbell rang, so Paul's feed had to be interrupted. He was put in his cot by his mother while she went into another room to be examined by the midwife. The observer was left to watch Paul. The interruption lasted altogether four minutes. It may have felt like an eternity to him. He started to cry and his crying escalated into screaming that drowned all conversation. It sounded as a protest and rage that could go on forever. As soon as the midwife had gone, Paul's mother picked him up and began to walk him about, talking to him, hoping to soothe him. He had soaked and dirtied himself in his fit of desperate explosive rage. The observer helped mother to collect some clean clothes. By now his crying tone had changed; it was softer. But although his mother was holding him and talking gently to him he seemed not to hear her voice. He resumed screaming when she put him down in an attempt to change him. He would not be comforted or calmed while this operation went on. She appeared worried and upset and said she had never heard him cry in that way. She held him close to her and soothed him, rocking him gently and telling him, "What a naughty mommy you have!" Finally he calmed down, but not without refusing the breast two more times, which added to his mother's "bad feelings."

This observation shows Paul in a state of disintegration that started the downward slide in a relationship that later on became sadomasochistic. The emotional storms in this baby proved to be too much for his mother to contain and transform. They were repeated with unusual and unbearable frequency, and Paul did not learn to tolerate even minimal frustrations. For her own pathological reasons, the mother refused all help offered to her and the baby. Eventually she defended herself by distancing more and more from an increasingly enraged and depressed baby. Paul withdrew into himself, and his development at eight months of age was severely impaired. He exhibited a series of somatic symptoms through which he was unconsciously trying to get the maternal attention he had lost. It was a tragic story.

In the case of Paul we can witness how the negative cycle of repeated events was determined by the particular violence of the deintegration–reintegration cycles, which always bordered on disintegration. Paul's frustration-tolerance was very limited and did not increase with the passage of time. He possessed an explosive temper. The notion of wait-ing and trusting that the breast would come was too hard for him to develop.

Paul could not come to terms with his mother's limitations; therefore he could not experience a good-enough mother/breast but remained encapsulated by the archetypal mother. His real mother could not help him enough. This is an example of how an infant's inability to create a maternal representation, because he cannot tolerate frustration, brings about somatic disturbances as the negative emotions concretely remain in the body and cause physical illness.

Barry

The following case is an extremely dramatic one, indicating what happens when a very depressed, angry, and unempathic mother is unable to respond to her baby's demands for cuddling and gentleness.

Barry is a very sensitive and potentially adaptable baby, born to a very deprived and hard young woman. Barry's mother is unable to tolerate any close, soft, intimate moments with her baby. She constantly pushes him away in an attempt to "toughen him up." Barry's father is a hard rock musician and the mother has lived in a world of hard rock music. Both parents are recovering alcoholics.

This young mother's mental representation of a baby boy is of a hard–phallic–macho guy who should not have any sensitive softness about him because she feels threatened by soft, tender feelings. She stopped being intimate with the baby after weaning him at about nine months. We have observed a positive relationship between the two, but we became aware that the situation started deteriorating when mother stopped breastfeeding him. It was as if she had enjoyed nursing him, and was resentful of his growing up and not needing her any longer for his survival in that way.

In the observation that follows, Barry is desperately trying to regain his lost "good mother," while continually being rejected by an angry, sarcastic mother. His frustrated expectations enrage him and he turns the rage against himself. He starts to bang his head, to scavenge food off the floor, and eventually starts striking his mother with hard blows. He was gradually becoming the "tough guy" who fit his mother's unconscious mental representation.

His negative experiences had been replicated time after time and his positive early expectations at the breast were fading away. It seemed as if he was banging his head against the wall of his mother's hard shell. Mother was increasingly acquiring the archetypal connotations of the bad mother – "the witch."

At the time this observation was recorded, Barry was seventeen and one half months old. Because of repeated experiences of rejection and his mother's sadistic teasing, he could not receive any comfort from her care. (Betty Harrison, Ph.D., recorded the observation.)

Mother opened the door to let me in. Barry was walking around the porch. I said "hi" to both of them, and we went into the living room. I sat down. Barry was walking around, and the TV was on. Mother said that Barry had been crabby all day. She went into the kitchen as she was saying this, putting the gate up behind her. Barry walked around the living room for a minute, picked up a book titled *The Busy Baby*, and handed it to me. Then he walked over to the gate, put his hands on it, tried to climb it, and began whining and crying. Mother asked him if he wanted grape juice; he continued to hang on to the gate, whining. She poured him some juice in a regular glass and stood there holding it on the other side of the gate, watching him cry and reach up to her, wanting to be picked up. After a little while, he took the juice, drank a little of it, and started walking towards me. I commented that he had a regular glass. Mother said she did that sometimes, mostly because his other cups were dirty. Barry came over to me, almost running, looking like he wanted me to pick him up. I caught his arm just before all of the grape juice went flying – some of it splashed me, some spilled on the floor. He looked disappointed that I didn't hug him, or pick him up. He noticed that I was concerned with the juice. I felt bad too, that I was worried about the juice and not focusing on him.

By this time mother had come and seen the juice spill. She got some cleaner to wipe it up, telling me that she had been jealous that her best friend had gotten all new furniture, but that after the juice spill the other day and now today, she was glad not to have new furniture. As she was cleaning, Barry was standing right behind her. She was scrubbing and wiping and, as she was finishing, Barry climbed up on the chair and sat on the spot she was cleaning. He sat there but did not look at mother – he was looking off in the distance. She told him that she needed to clean where he was sitting – he did not respond. Then she said something to me about how she and Barry were talking different languages that day. As soon as she was done, she went back into the kitchen.

Barry went over to the gate, again trying to climb it, crying, screaming, and whining, and reaching out for mother. Barry lay down on the floor, clanking his head as he lay back. Mother said, "Oh, that was dramatic." For the next ten minutes or so, he lay there on the floor, crying and whimpering. He rolled over on his side. For a while he was under the table leaning against the wall, sometimes whimpering, sometimes just sitting. His eyes began to close several times. At one point mother said to him that this was just pathetic. Mother had told me earlier that he had gotten up early and had not taken a nap that day. He was lying in the corner, by the gate, whimpering. At one point he became distracted by something on the wall, then after a minute started crying again. I thought he was going to fall asleep, but he didn't. He just lay on the floor, half crying.

Finally Barry got up and again went over to the gate, arms out, crying. This time mother opened the gate and picked him up, holding him against her, and he molded into her shoulder. Immediately she went over to the TV, holding Barry, asking him if he wanted to watch Batman. She changed the channel and then sat down with him on the couch and they started watching TV. Barry tried climbing into her lap, but she pushed him back and pointed to the TV, saying "Batman."

Barry climbed into mother's lap and this time she allowed it. She said, "Let's show Betty all of your new tricks." She had told me earlier that just in the past week Barry had learned many new words, and that he could point to his eyes, ears, hair, mouth, and "Buddha belly." Barry was facing mother, sitting in her lap, and she was trying to get him to touch his hair, eyes, etc. She was asking him where things were, and he was pointing to her eyes, putting his fingers in them. He held on her nose, hard, she said, "Honk." She asked him where his Buddha belly was and he started slapping her breasts. She was saying, no, she didn't have a Buddha belly, only babies had Buddha bellies and was patting his stomach, making it a game. Then Barry hit mother, hard, in the face. She grabbed his hand, saying, "Not like this; be soft." This sequence of distress and despair in Barry is difficult to tolerate. Mother is constantly criticizing him, belittling him, and teasing him for his attempts to get close to her and be comforted. He is left to scream on his own on the floor. There is no compassion or helpful intervention on the part of the mother, who treats his distress as a sort of hysterical fit. She has put a barrier between herself and the child of which the gate is a concrete representation. She cannot tolerate him close to her, but he keeps trying. After many failed attempts he falls on the floor exhausted and hopeless, to which the mother responds by picking him up and briefly holding him. He molds himself into her arms ready to make up with her. Here, the memory of the earlier good feeding still supports Barry, allowing him to hold on to a loving feeling for his mother. But the mother cannot tolerate the affectionate gesture and puts him down again. When finally Barry loses control and begins to hit her breasts harder and harder, Mother stops him and finally caresses him telling him that he must be gentle, just like that, and she strokes him.

It seems to me that only when the boy has turned into a harsh, violent aggressor does she stop her tormenting behavior and become soft. By her repeated tormenting and distancing actions, Mother teaches Barry to become harsh and violent with her. And Barry, in spite of his desire to have a loving relationship with her, has to resort to hurting his mother to get her to respond to his needs. Thus we observe in this case how replication of negative behavior on the mother's part, caused by her own pathology, has created a serious disturbance in the child.

Discussion

I have emphasized the essential function of replication for learning. Without repetition, no learning can occur. In this learning process, repeated good experiences counteract repeated bad ones, and if the good experiences outnumber the bad ones, a healthy enough emotional development can take place. However, the repetition of negative experiences, which constellate the negative aspect of the mother archetype, contributes to the development of severe pathologies. Further, repetition as a compulsion can also be used by the infant to defend itself against change, and ultimately against growth.

In my view, it is important to study those aspects of infant development that could be defined as archetypal. We encounter these in the deintegration–reintegration patterns of the infant.

As we have seen in the above case observations, when these patterns relate to the mother they challenge her ego strength and her capacity to adapt to her infant's needs without falling prey to rigid or negative unconscious representations.

When we become aware of the complexities and the risk factors inherent in early mother–infant relationships, we can appreciate the miracle of healthy development. By observing infant–parent interaction we become more aware of how dysfunctional interaction sets in. Consequently, if we were able to intervene at an early stage, many severe disturbances could be prevented by setting in motion a cycle of positive repetitive reinforcements that will prevent a pathological cycle from developing.

Finally, we must keep in mind that there is no one way to approach such therapeutic interventions. Although it may be true that all of us share a certain ontological collectivity, each individual is unique and interprets and responds in his own way to his experience.

Chapter 4

Naming the nameless

A way to stop acting out

In this chapter I focus on acting out as a way of communicating unnamed, unprocessed primitive material that has neither undergone transformation nor acquired symbolic representation. I will discuss the cases of two adolescent boys with severe unconscious fantasies of suicide.

Two adolescents in a rage

In his recent paper "Jung's Infancy and Childhood and Its Influence upon the Development of Analytical Psychology," Brian Feldman wrote:

> While Jung's early experiences had mainly an ecstatic emotional quality, this emotional tone may have been a defense against a particular painful affect. The source of this pain was apparently the significant problems with Jung's family. When Jung was three years old, his mother was hospitalized for what appears to have been a severe depression. She was away from the child for several months. During that time, he was taken care of by a maid.
>
> At that time Jung developed a severe skin rash which he later on connected with the separation of his parents and his mother's separation. It is probable that the skin eczema was related to the sense of psychic catastrophe which Jung experienced subsequent to his separation from his mother. It was as if he were unable to contain torturous emotions within himself and they burst out in somatic form.
>
> (Feldman 1992: 262)

Then Feldman quotes Jung:

> "I was deeply troubled by my mother being away. From then on I always felt mistrustful when the word love was spoken. The feeling I associated with woman was for a long time that of innate unreliability."

Feldman continues:

> I think that the passage quoted above may help us in understanding the origins of Jung's difficulties in his emotional relationship with women; his need to make sense of the nonsense of his mother's breakdown and long absence, and the pain that it caused him, for which it seems that he received no emotional help at the time, and by which he was "deeply troubled"! He seems to have experienced his mother's hospitalization as a betrayal which led him to be "always mistrustful when the word love was spoken."
>   The question is: could baby Jung have been helped in making sense of his mother's illness? Could he have been made to understand that her leaving him was not a betrayal? Did anyone tell him that his mother loved him, that she was miserable because she had to go away, and that she was aware of the pain and panic her departure caused him? What part did this early abandonment contribute to his difficulties and his own breakdown in later life and could it have been alleviated by someone talking to him about it? It is difficult to say a posteriori, but early dramatic experiences of the sort he underwent are a significant factor in the activation of early splitting defense mechanisms.
>
>   (Feldman 1992: 263)

My two patients, Andrew and Anthony, in my view did not receive sufficient contingent maternal support to make sense of their experiences as small children. Thus parts of their personalities remained in a state of confusion, panic, and despair.

Andrew

Autistic – Do Not Speak
My words are lost shouts in a dead prison, torn assemblages of
    thoughts in a mute body,
Or dust in the air that breathed then.
My words are stones sweeping the beach,

The pebbles thrown carelessly by innocent children,
Sinking. Swept away by the tide.
All worn and inadequate communications
Broken mirror: Darkened windows.
Empty shells on the shore. You can hear the sea.
But I who is words, untrained passion and solitude,
I am unaccessible, unexpressable, floating unwritable thoughts,
They are my movements and my body. . .

Andrew was an articulate and sophisticated seventeen-year-old. He came from an educated, intellectual family. His mother was a doctor of medicine and his father a university professor. Everyone in his family was highly intelligent and articulate, and knowledge meant everything to them. Andrew had one older brother.

When Andrew first came to me, after having rejected another therapist, he was suicidal and greatly distressed, but for many sessions he kept up a steady stream of cool, sophisticated, and matter-of-fact conversation about education, literature, and theater, which were his hobbies. He was bright, entertaining, and witty. He spoke at great speed without ever losing the flow of the conversation, as if he were afraid of letting go of the ball for fear of losing it to the other team or not scoring. His words flowed endlessly, as if intent on leaving no gaps, no empty spaces during which he might catch a glimpse of his own distress and loneliness. He seemed to be keeping himself together by stringing interminable chains of words, while his body sat stiffly in his chair, like a wooden puppet.

Andrew's use of language seemed to have a defensive quality to it right from the start. I believe that his lively conversation had several aims: one was to make himself interesting and to communicate his ideas; another, less conscious one was aimed at concealing his feelings of vulnerability and inferiority.

Could his need to develop mastery of language from an early stage have emanated from his need to be understood by his intellectual and professional mother? Did baby Andrew use words to reach his mother in order to involve her with him? He also used sounds as autistic objects in order to make himself feel alive. Sometimes he used words as empty shells, merely for decoration; at other times, he used words as "stuffers," to fill up empty gaps of time and space between us, especially when he felt in danger of falling into a frightening hole where his shouts and screams would get lost. The early internalized mother was a non-containing, non-soothing "dead prison" in his mind.

In my countertransference, it became clear to me that I was not expected to absorb, contain, or hear anything he was telling me. I felt he behaved as if I were not there, as if he were talking to himself in a sort of masturbatory way, puffing himself up, listening with obvious pleasure to the sound of his own voice and showing off his verbal acrobatics. Through my feeling of being shut off by him, I could be in touch with his sense of hopeless loneliness.

In oedipal terms, his stiff body posture suggested that the boy was in a permanent state of erection with emotions/meaning attached to it, as if in his adolescent mind he was still unable to make sense of these bodily feelings and emotions for which the early mother had not provided a containing name.

Right from the start I was struck by the split between the animation in his voice, the liveliness of his speech, and the lifeless rigidity of his limbs. At the beginning, he hardly ever moved in his chair. He often sounded like a headmaster reporting, with poise and superior arrogance, on the problems he was having with one of his students. The "headmaster" was a personification of a stereotyped rigidity that he was trying to emulate and was criticizing at the same time. When he allowed his adolescent self to come through, he also attacked the stiff persona, which he mistakenly identified with "adult behavior."

It seemed as if the male role model offered him by both the headmaster and his own father, the university professor, had a rigid quality to which his own personality could not adapt, in spite of his sincere attempts to fit in with their demands. He was a playful, lively child who had been mercilessly repressed and undermined. This repression was partly a collective repression, due to the British educational system in which he had been raised. But it became clear to me that his personality would never fit into that particular mold without great loss of creativity and joy of life.

On the other hand, his connection with his mother as a small child had also lacked closeness and warmth, due in part to her own personality and to the fact that for long periods of time he had been left with a variety of caretakers while his mother was at work.

He did have a good, warm connection with a grandmother, as well as – later on – with his father, who used to spend a lot of time at home writing. Yet even then he was not allowed to go talk to him or to disturb him with his boisterous, enthusiastic stories, because the father needed quiet for his work.

All of this became slowly clearer to me through his talking and my observation of him, session after session. While he was swamping me with his endless speech, I had to hold on to my thoughts. Often I found myself thinking, "After all, there is nothing wrong with this young man; he is okay." Then, however, I would remember that this same young man had tried to commit suicide. Obviously, I was getting caught up in his splitting. He wore the conversational persona as a mask and wanted to make me and everyone else believe that, indeed, he was all right. Unfortunately for him, the same defensive system was operative in the very culture in which he lived. Thus, he had to go a long way before his despair could come to the fore and manifest itself in the suicidal behavior. The feelings which he described in the poem slowly became available to be worked on in the analytic sessions, and in my work with him I concentrated on the analysis of the material with a particular focus on the pre-oedipal aspects. Thanks to our work together, he was finally able to feel the depth of the split within which he was operating, as well as make sense of and give a name to his deepest emotions. These emotions were all the more disturbing because he never knew that they were there. They were "movements in my body," nonspecific discharge of restless discomfort.

These inexpressible states of discomfort are, in my view, related to untransformed early infantile experiences which have not been made sense of, primarily by the mother, in the dyadic relationship. The empathic tuning-in with the infant on the part of the mother and her maternal care has two aspects: one is the physical attending to the baby's body, the other is the attending to the baby's emotional needs. The empathic tuning-in on the part of the mother usually alleviates the infant's sense of impotence by promptly meeting his needs in a manner that the infant can experience as "magical" or "miraculous."

Although this process sounds complex, most mothers are naturally able to perform this function and, on the whole, these complex interactions take place in an average way within most mother–baby dyads. But a variety of factors may hamper the smooth development of this mutuality: illnesses, deaths in the family, and premature separations of mother and baby (like his mother returning to work too soon, as in the case of my young patient).

In my view, which was confirmed by my countertransference, Andrew's mother was only partially able to decode the nonverbal communications of her baby. Often in the sessions I felt like a baby, completely nonexistent; he was constantly talking above my head. I felt undermined, uninteresting, as if he were not paying attention to my words. I felt frustrated and ignored, just as baby Andrew must have felt, unable to communicate his feelings to his mother.

The feelings that he evoked in me were those that he had kept inside himself, raw, unprocessed, and loaded with violent emotions of which he was unaware. In his analysis, he kept projecting these feelings onto a girlfriend, his headmaster, and me. These primitive, unintegrated parts of himself re-emerged due to the developmental crisis of adolescence (the deintegration of adolescence, according to Fordham) and had started exerting pressure on his ego and needed to be integrated.

At first, Andrew had tried to deal with the problem by using the splitting mechanisms by which he had operated in those areas since infancy. However, with the energy liberated by the upsurge of adolescence, his earlier mechanisms could no longer protect him from the painful, distressing feelings that had been locked up in the unconscious meandering of his bodily experience. The last lines of his poem describe this state of affairs very well: "I am unaccessible, unexpressable, floating unwritable thoughts. They are my movements and my body . . ."

However, he wrote the poem I have quoted here in the third year of his therapy. Only then was he able to express the state he had been in and give it a name. At the beginning of the therapy, he appeared to want to impress me with his manners, his intellectual and verbal abilities, and most of all he wanted me to treat him as an equal. In this way he would be just as attractive as any oedipal rival, like his brother, his father, or any of my other male patients. In reality, he felt he was the least "interesting one," the baby with the small penis in whom either his mother or I could not possibly be interested. On the other hand, as a defense, he had adopted the "stuck up" grown-up behavior which had made him very unpopular with his peer group, as he "acted grown up and arrogant towards them." In relation to me, I think that he had wanted to distract me, to make me find him interesting, an equal, a man with a "big penis" like his father, thus using oedipal fantasies to cover up earlier infantile ones in relation to the pre-oedipal mother and her early abandonment. His experience had been of having to hide and strap in the part of himself which felt "inaccessible and unexpressable."

As I mentioned, I could only vaguely intuit this state of affairs when he first came to see me, but many images of bleak, derelict, empty houses appeared in his dreams at the onset of his therapy. He also complained of feeling bored and lonely and of spending a great deal of time locked up in his room alone, listening to loud rock music. He had managed to split off his worst feelings, projecting them onto a girlfriend who had tried to kill herself, and he had become very concerned on her behalf. We spent many sessions in which he described his girlfriend's extreme feelings of emptiness, despair, and loneliness. He depicted her household as cold and bleak and said that nobody loved *her* at home.

The more he progressed in the description of the girlfriend's emotional state, the more I would become aware of him projecting his vulnerable, infantile, distressed part onto her. But it took a long time for him to be able to see what he was doing. I also felt that in the transference he needed to experience me as a mother/girlfriend who could engage with him emotionally, understand him, and contain him without falling apart.

However, the transference of his sexual fantasies into me, mother/girlfriend, aroused great anxieties and excited bodily feelings in him, as whenever he talked about his girlfriend in the session, he could no longer maintain his rigid body posture. He would become agitated and begin to move his body with jerky restlessness on the chair. He interspersed the descriptions of the girlfriend with reports of his activity in school and his teacher's complaints about his "noisy restlessness," which disturbed the lessons.

An interesting coincidence occurred when another patient of mine accidentally broke the chair in which Andrew sat during sessions, and I had to send it out for repair. Andrew immediately noticed the disappearance of "his" chair but did not verbalize it. Instead, he exhibited a distressed state which he could not attribute to anything that had happened to him. He looked anxious, became completely stiff, appeared agitated and unable to sit comfortably; I pointed this out to him, but he was unable to make sense of what was going on. This behavior carried on for a couple of sessions during which he regressed considerably, looking insecure and depressed, and complaining that he did not know what was going on with him. At the same time, he seemed to scan me with the greatest attention, to control my every movement, as if he were expecting some dangerous reaction from me.

Actually, I thought that the disappearance of "his" chair (and the unconscious meaning that it had for the infantile part of him) might have been the factor that had caused his regression. At an oedipal level, his reaction might have also been caused by the fantasy that a male rival had been inside me in his place.

I interpreted that it seemed to me what he was feeling was related to his unconscious anxiety about having destroyed my chair or me. He feared being a bad, destructive boy, like as an infant he had feared having destroyed his mother's lap, which caused his mother to go away, and he had felt abandoned and desperate. And now he was afraid that he had damaged me, too, and that I would abandon him also. At first, he verbally rejected my interpretation; but his body immediately began to loosen up. He sat more comfortably, leaning back into the chair, and all his body tension disappeared. He resumed his lively conversation and seemed to enjoy the remaining part of the session.

It was only some sessions later that he was able to tell me that I was right. He *had* worried about the chair. He was afraid that I would get angry, and that my husband (the oedipal rival) would get angry with him, too, and that we might ask his parents to pay for the damage. The same thing used to happen at school, where his parents were constantly called in to hear complaints about his lack of discipline.

The episode of the broken chair and his regression and panic reaction in the transference made it possible for me to have a reverie and fantasy about how he had felt as a small child, apparently blaming himself for his mother leaving him. It also brought into the open his fear of his father's anger and punishment for his misbehavior.

In the countertransference I felt his pre-oedipal fear and panic at the thought of having damaged the mother/analyst's lap/chair, mixed with his castration anxieties about the revenge of the oedipal father (my husband). By interpreting these feelings to him and naming them, I helped him to make sense of nameless emotions, which had remained raw and unprocessed because his mother had been unable to tune in and give a name to the negative feelings that he had experienced as a baby when she had returned prematurely to work.

Thanks to the transformation produced by the naming of the emotional state of the past, which gave relief in the present, the experience became digestible, and Andrew slowly began to make sense of his early history as distinct from the present.

A few months before his therapy ended, after his final exams, Andrew decided to go on a trip to the Far East, which we understood as being his initiation quest. The trip went well. Here is a passage from a letter he wrote to me from India:

> No one hustles or feels the need to rush about – this is partly to do with the heat . . . however, I have felt a new kind of stillness and see the beauty of waiting with the right mind of being calm and serene. This only leaves the problem of how to balance this with my more boisterous side. I have not found it particularly easy to be away from home. I feel that I have done only so that I can be welcomed back and thereby judge their love for me. However, on the other hand, there have been times again when I have felt stronger than I

have ever done before – being almost alone and winning – I am able to cope with this, though I am occupied more with new ideas from the very Indians I have talked to on trains.

In this letter Andrew was reassuring me that he was okay in spite of the hardships that he was having to face in his journey. He also acknowledged to himself that he missed his family and me, and that being away from the home he had complained about was a mixed blessing. He realized he loved his parents and me and regretted being away, although he had to for his own needs. He was telling me that moving away and separating both from me and his parents was not just the "good riddance" experience which he had fantasized about, but by being away he could miss the good aspects of home and therapy and enjoy the idea of coming back.

This meant to me that he was now really ready to leave therapy as he had reached the ability to experience grief, and he could tell me about it.

The ability to communicate with words is a specifically human quality, which is slowly developed in the first two years of life. To be able to use words and language is the first step in the process of symbolization by which a person or a thing is called and designated as distinct from another person or thing. It is the only way by which one's personal experience can be made accessible and transmitted to other human beings, by the use of a shared symbolic code.

Before words begin to exist as a means to express oneself, sounds and actions have to be used to make oneself understood. From birth, babies address themselves to their mothers and/or parents expecting to be understood and have their needs met, and they are endowed with a variety of facial expressions and gestures to communicate their emotions and interest. On their part, the parents have the difficult task of helping to translate into language these nonverbal communications. The function of helping the baby put into words his experiences and give them a name is a very complex one which demands empathic tuning-in on the part of the adult. By helping the baby to find words for experiences and emotions as yet unnamed by him, the mother facilitates the baby's dialogue with the world, as the baby can share more effectively his feelings, needs, and thoughts.

Under normal circumstances, a baby is able to make sense of his experiences and to receive support from his mother in states of anxiety, pain, distress, or whenever he feels overwhelmed by frustration and fear. However, there are great differences in babies and their inborn capacities as well as in mothers and their mothering abilities and their sensitivity to the baby's communications and needs.

There are circumstances in which the flow of communication and emotional exchange between mother and baby are disturbed for a variety of reasons, such as the baby's fragility, or the mother's insensitivity, or external events such as traumas, premature separations, illnesses, or death. In these cases, those areas of emotional experiences often remain unnamed because the baby has no words for them.

In order for the mother to experience this "reverie," she has to be able to make space inside herself for the baby's emotional evacuations. She needs to contain them, sort them out, and return them to him enriched with meaning. However, many factors may hamper this process. If the mother is depressed or ill, or her mind is taken up with preoccupations and worries of all sorts originating from her family or working life, she will not be able to dedicate to her infant the amount of reverie that he needs. This in turn will lead to difficulties in tuning in to her baby's non-verbal communications.

One might say that, for instance, in the case of Jung, when the maternal "reverie" failed to perform the transformation for the baby, the beta elements remained raw and primitive and manifested themselves as disturbing, unintegrated "crazy parts" in an otherwise functioning psyche. These (psychotic) beta elements are often not verbalizable and manifest themselves in somatic form as well as in uncontainable affects and grandiose fantasies. In Jungian terms, we may say that these primitive elements – which he called "psychoid" – have remained in an asymbolic, unnamed form.

On the other hand, I believe that the fundamental function of the analyst, when working with regressed patients, consists of helping them to name and make sense of these primitive unnamed elements (Bion's beta elements), which block and disturb their emotional development. In so doing, the analyst can be helped greatly by countertransference reactions and emotions.

In my own work, I am very attentive to nonverbal bodily communications on the part of the patient as well as to my own countertransference reaction to those nonverbal communications, in order to try to penetrate the misty area of preverbal interaction and relatedness. To do this, one needs to focus one's attention on every minute detail of the session. Not only does one need to listen to all the verbal communications and silences, one needs also to perceive all the changes taking place in the patient's body, such as vitality levels, breathing patterns, tension levels, and voice changes. One needs to let oneself be tuned in with them in one's own body in order to relate them to the emotional states of which the patient himself is not conscious. From the subsequent reflection and evaluation of all the data thus collected, the analyst will hopefully be able to construct a useful interpretation in due time. My second case history will illustrate further definite noncontingency on the part of the mother in relation to the patient's infant self.

Anthony

Another variable is the actual age of the child when abandonment is experienced, when coming to understand how things went wrong. Also, the position in the family is important in understanding how feelings of self-esteem or lack of them may complicate the situation in relation to narcissistic injury. For instance, Andrew felt that he was the youngest, least significant member of his family, whereas Anthony was put up for adoption by his birth mother, which made him more vulnerable.

A colleague told me that I would receive a call by a distressed father whose sixteen-year-old son had run away from home for two weeks. Could I help if when he came back they would bring him to see me? So a week later Anthony appeared accompanied by his mother. I was struck by his unusual looks. He was Asian with a Rastafarian hairstyle which conveyed to me his identity problem. His adoptive parents were British who had lived in Asia and had adopted him as a baby. He apparently had been a perfect child, making his parents happy till the parents divorced when he was eight and they moved to the United States. But the real trouble had begun when they both remarried and the father had a little girl. By then Anthony had reached adolescence and had started acting out. His mother appeared very depressed and worn out. The father, whom I subsequently met, was a top executive who appeared to be very angry at Anthony for his behavior and very rigid in his views and expectations for his son. Psychological and emotional factors did not count for him.

Anthony, in his rageful acting out, aimed at defying the very same establishment that his father valued by becoming involved in gang activity and being caught by the police several times.

He also wanted to punish his mother, whom he admitted he dearly loved, because her alcoholic second husband apparently abused her and was prejudiced against Anthony. He told me he also hated his step-mother, who was rigid and strict, always telling him off and praising his stepsister.

I was struck by Anthony's appearance. He was very handsome and had a charismatic style about himself in his identification with a rebel hero. He was a mixture of a samurai and a black panther. He definitely wanted to scare me and let me know that he was a tough, fearless guy, and the business of going into therapy was his mother's idea.

I listened to his enraged tirades against his parents and step-parents and told him that I could understand his rage because he felt he had lost his home, which had now been invaded by those step-parents who rejected him and made his life miserable and that was why he ran away. There were more rageful protests in a pseudo-cool tone as if to say, "You think I fall for that clever crap?"

Then his protest turned against the school, where he said he was persecuted for his ethnicity. To show the bullies who he was he had joined the fiercest gang of colored thugs, so now they would leave him alone because his friends had guns and were not afraid to shoot.

He carried on saying that he did not fear the police either. He and his friends enjoyed speeding and having a police car chase them. At this point I asked him, why did he want to be killed? He shrugged his shoulders and said he did not care, then added that the gang leader was very fierce because he had no family.

I began to fear for his life and I told him so, I said also that I had no power to stop him committing suicide but I felt that with his natural gifts he could do better.

At the end of the session he left with no guarantee that he would come back.

That same night I could not sleep out of concern and fear of what could happen to him. I had introjected his deeply unconscious projective identification. While he consciously did not feel fear and panic, yet he was terrified for his life and wanted to be rescued by me, perhaps a repeat of the infantile dread from which he was rescued by his adoptive parents. I realized how uncontainable he was.

When he arrived late after having again been kicked out of school and having been arrested for gang-related activities, I told him that given his present situation he needed a safe boarding school because I feared he would get shot. He sat throughout the session with a defiant look on his face, denied being in trouble or afraid. His acting out increased in the following weeks.

He stopped coming to therapy and ran away. During that time I had frequent meetings with his parents, who agreed to send him to boarding school abroad when he came back. Luckily he agreed to go.

Three months later he had settled down and was happy there. He wrote to his mother thanking her and me for having saved his life.

My training as an analyst combined with my experience of real infants, but mainly my countertransference reactions, helped me to tune in to these patients' early needs and anxieties which had remained split off and unknown to their adult egos. Thus I was able to perform the reverie that their mothers had not; that is to say, I experienced within myself their chaotic, primitive emotions, recognized them in myself, and named them to my patients.

Chapter 5

Defense of the self in a case of severe deprivation

Drawing on material from analytic sessions with a severely traumatized young boy, I explore in this chapter the connection between early emotional deprivation and the resultant mental representations of this deprivation in the inner world of the child. I attempt to demonstrate that the terrifying archetypal imagery I encountered in my work with this boy was rooted in experiences that occurred in his infancy, experiences that included maternal neglect compounded by early hospitalization and subsequent parental abandonment. I found that the boy lived in a world dominated by bizarre archetypal fantasies and persecutory hallucinations, along with the population of monsters and hostile space aliens intent on destroying him. I illustrate the process of transformation that took place in the transference–countertransference relationship, a process that led him out of his mechanical, archetypal world into a human reality.

Living in a crazy world

Seven-year-old Peter was referred to me for therapy by a child psychiatrist who had treated him for a short time. Peter had been referred to the psychiatrist by a local hospital. The presenting symptoms were extreme hyperactivity, confusion, and senseless talk. Peter held loud conversations with imaginary beings and made loud anal farts as well as farting noises with his mouth whenever he became anxious or angry. He was also encopretic under stress.

Peter had been fostered by his present family from age three and a half months, and finally adopted at age six. Reports from the adoptive parents indicate that up until six months of age, he had exhibited signs of severe failure-to-thrive, crying constantly and vomiting excessively. His father reported having to feed him with a dropper because he vomited almost all his food. At birth, Peter's weight had been very low. He had been born to an adolescent mother who apparently had abused alcohol and perhaps drugs during her pregnancy. The natural parents were both very young and emotionally unstable. The mother was described as being below average in intelligence and unable to bond with her babies. Peter had a brother ten months older, who suffered the same neglect as did Peter. The parents divorced soon after Peter was born, and the father moved to another state and cut off all contact. This made the mother's already precarious caring abilities deteriorate further. Immediately after birth Peter developed a serious respiratory tract infection and was hospitalized for a couple of weeks. His physical problems continued throughout his childhood. By the age of six he had had surgery every year: hernia, tonsils, adenoids, and on one occasion tubes had to be installed in his ears. When he returned to his mother after the first hospitalization, he had cried constantly. The mother could not cope with his distress. She was erratic in her caring for both babies, and lonely and depressed after the divorce. Driven mad by Peter's constant screaming, she locked him in a closet so as not to hear him. Finally, alerted by the neighbors, social services intervened and both children were taken into care.

Peter was switched from one foster home to another because no one could tolerate his screaming. Finally, at age three and a half months, he was placed with his present family. These early experiences – loss of his mother, physical pain, neglect, isolation in the hospital – all contributed to the constellation of a hostile and persecutory world/breast for him.

In spite of the adverse circumstances of Peter's life and his severe pathology, his personality is endowed with considerable vitality, resilience, and hopefulness. These attributes have allowed him finally to bond with his adoptive parents and with me.

Peter's adoptive parents are committed, well-meaning, religious people. However, they are burdened with their own unresolved personal problems, and are psychologically unsophisticated. They fostered several children before Peter came to stay with them as well as during the time Peter was in their care. Finally, having become attached to him, they adopted him. Both parents are scientists, and their professional commitments require that they travel frequently. These periodic departures aggravated Peter's fears of abandonment. Peter would become extremely upset when one of his parents was away. The parents, used to dealing in a world of concrete facts, were both defensive and uncomprehending about these separation anxieties. Their work schedules necessitated that Peter be taken to day care. He then had to be moved from one placement to another because of his inconsolable crying, ferocious tantrums, aggressive behavior to the other children, and regressive soiling of his pants.

Since the parents fostered other children, the comings and goings of these children undoubtedly threatened Peter's stability. One little girl stayed long enough for Peter to think of her as a sister and become attached to her. However, she was even more disturbed than Peter, and the parents could not cope with her. She was returned to social services. This episode, which happened shortly before Peter was referred to me, increased his symptoms of soiling and aggressive behavior. (I have often wondered what criteria social services use that result in placing needy, disturbed children in the care of foster parents busy with full-time jobs and travel. And what function do these children have for such foster parents? But these questions are beyond the scope of this book.)

Clearly, such behavior was the result of Peter's fear that he too would be sent away. His anxiety made him act to test his parents' commitment to him. In total exasperation, they decided to send Peter for psychotherapy. But they had determined that, if the therapy was not effective, they would have to send him away, despite their attachment to him.

The child psychiatrist had prescribed Ritalin for Peter's hyperactivity. However, the medicine had little result. From Peter's bizarre behavior in our early sessions, I suspected a psychosis.

As is my practice, I saw Peter alone to make an assessment of his condition, and then saw his parents. When I first encountered him, he looked small and underdeveloped for his age, more like a five-year-old than his actual age of seven. He appeared lively and alert, and indeed very hyperactive. He could not keep still. He could be very verbal, and yet his speech could also become very confused. He made noises like someone afflicted by Gilles de la Tourette's syndrome. However, there was a soft and gentle side to his nature. He had beautiful eyes and an endearing smile, and he soon convinced me he was very bright. As the therapy progressed, I discovered he had a generous side to him, and a good sense of humor. Even though I liked him immediately, I realized that our working together would bring some extremely difficult times.

Peter spent the whole first hour crawling at my feet, examining a box of toys. He took all the toys out of the box and scattered them, throwing them around the room in a frantic, senseless way. While doing this, he made noises as if bombs were exploding and blowing everything apart. At the end of the hour, my room was full of the debris from these explosions, and all the toys were broken.

While scattering and exploding the toys, Peter seemed immersed in a deep fantasy – unreachable, as if in a trance. At the end of the session he asked me to put all the broken toys away, and told me he would fix everything next time. When I told him the session was over, he went quite willingly. And when I mentioned that I would be seeing his parents the next week, he did not protest.

The following session Peter carried on the game of explosion, this time accompanied by strong farting noises. The noises prevailed over talk. I made my first interpretation and said that so far he had shown me how quickly he could fall apart. It was clear that he felt exploded, uncontained, and disintegrated. I added that it seemed to me that he was feeling very much like the broken little toys, and I suggested that maybe by working together we could find out more about these broken feelings and fix them for him. He was willing to accept my offer. Given all the professionals he had seen only briefly in the past, I told him that I would be seeing him for a long time. I wondered what he made of my statement, but he started coming regularly and eagerly to his sessions. The sessions were once a week. He lived far away, and his parents had to drive him to see me after school. They found these appointments very demanding, and they alternated bringing him each week. However, seeing Peter once a week was not enough, and I increased the number of sessions per week as soon as it was possible.

For the first six months of therapy, Peter was extremely manic and mostly did not relate to me. He presented very interesting play fantasies. He appeared to use them as hallucinations, as if I were not in the room with him. He seemed to expect to be alone and used these hallucinations to comfort himself, in the way a young infant might comfort himself in the absence of the mother. In time, though, he began to say to me, "Let's pretend," and tried to involve me more in his play activity. However, as soon as I became involved, he would take off on his own and ignore me completely. While this lasted, he became as if possessed by the toy-scattering activity. Gradually his play changed, and he began to include the furniture and my body as elements of his game.

The spaceship

I saw Peter in my adult consulting room, where there are two armchairs, a couch, a bookshelf, and a table desk with a plastic top for him to draw on. There are also several cushions, which he used to build a spaceship. I would sit in my chair and he would place cushions in front of my legs, sit against them, and then place others on either side to create a sort of containing space. Then, using my foot as a control panel, he would say that he was the pilot and we were in a spaceship flying to outer space. This game was repeated for several months. We had to fight attacking aliens in enemy spaceships equipped with lethal weapons. This battle against the persecuting aliens that surrounded us was extremely dangerous. We had to shoot the aliens and then explode their ships in mid-air before they reached us. At the same time we had to avoid collision with the debris of exploded ships that was floating in space. Peter appointed me his assistant and equipped me with an endless number of space guns with which I was supposed to protect and rescue him. I felt that I had to function as a mother/father allied to his ego that was fighting for its survival. I could see this as the beginning of a positive therapeutic alliance.

Most of the time during this play, Peter was in a state of acute persecution. The alien persecutory elements, derived from archetypal imagery – to use a Jungian term – invaded his internal space. One might also say – to use Bion's terminology – that unmetabolized beta elements had invaded his internal space. Although these terms are not identical, both point to undigested primary emotional experiences that occurred in infancy and terrified the infant's ego. When an infant feels overwhelmed by such affects, and the mother is unable to make sense of them for him, he will try to expel these feelings by projecting them onto an external object, usually the mother. In the absence of good-enough processing by the mother (see Bion's concept of maternal reverie (Bion 1967: 116)), the emotional contents that had been expelled by the infant are reintrojected as persecutory elements. These mechanisms were very active in Peter's sessions. As is often the case with much younger children, the internal persecutory contents are experienced as concrete (not symbolic or metaphorical), and as objectively coming from the outer world.

Peter's persecutory states made me speculate on the vicissitudes of his early history. These had added an element of concrete reality to his inner fantasies. His low birth weight, his early severe respiratory illness, his hospitalizations and surgeries, his persistent crying, and then his abandonment by his mother – all conspired to make him feel that no-one could tolerate the "badness" of his negative feelings. No one had helped him deal with these feelings, and therefore they had possessed him and driven him crazy. Not only did he feel he was bad, he did his best to convince everyone around him that he *was* bad.

When Peter was in his persecutory states, his communications were extremely difficult to comprehend; they consisted mostly of noises, screams, and farts. His ego, disintegrating under the attack of the aliens, would regress to an infant modality that led him eventually to soil himself. I think that the familiar smell of his farts was comforting to him in the sense of "going-on-being," as described by Winnicott. He appeared completely possessed by his violent fantasy world. I believe that his hyperactivity served the function of maintaining a level of hyper-alertness that he imagined was needed to protect his infant self from being destroyed in the absence of maternal care.

It was almost impossible for me to think in the midst of this chaos. In the countertransference, I switched between feeling so alienated at the center of this war zone that I wanted to scream at him to stop, and then wanting to take him in my arms and protect him as if he were an actual infant under imminent attack. Every now and then in the course of his play, he would turn to me and order me to execute some landing or take-off maneuver, since he was so busy shooting for dear life. At the end of each session he would say, "We shall continue next time," and rush off to throw himself into his parent's lap. Although he showed some resistance to leaving the sessions at this stage in his therapy, the real opposition surfaced later on as a result of his attachment to me.

During this period, I was not allowed to speak or make interpretations. If I tried, Peter treated my words as if they were alien bullets, although he wanted my presence there all the time. Once, in the heat of battle, he shouted at the aliens, "I've got my mother here helping me out!" At this point I said he was trying to scare the aliens with my presence, and that he felt I was a supportive ally. I was like a mother with a young infant, unlike when he was a baby and his mother could not be there to shelter and protect him from alien attacks.

In response, he started screaming and fighting my interpretation with all his breath. It was obvious that my words had disturbed his grandiose fantasies and had threatened his defense system. My comments in relation to him as an infant made him feel very anxious, and he defended himself by jumping up and down, screaming, and farting in a state of confusion and panic. This manic reaction was also a way in which the most destructive part of his personality could resist and destroy the nourishment provided by my interpretation as well as his own potential capacity for assimilating "good food." Thus the cycle of deprivation, distress, and isolation could not be relieved.

Slowly, however, the space wars began to give way to other games. Peter built a paper track for racing cars. The speeding cars would quickly get out of control, jumping all obstacles and flying through the air, then crashing down and eventually breaking into pieces. The early game of space disasters was now being played out on earth. The violence and speed of the races made him excited and aggressive, and he accompanied the game with exhaust sounds and farts. He exhibited a perverse pleasure each time a car turned over and broke. The game seemed to express the enormous resistance that he, like the car driver, had to overcome in order to reduce his manic mental speed so that his mental activity would not fragment and disintegrate.

I interpreted the game to Peter. I told him the drivers of the little cars were always driving much too fast, just as he drove himself when he became frantic. And, just like him, the drivers could never win the race because they would become too agitated and lose control. I added that he, too, had difficulties in containing himself and gaining control of his emotions in response to my interpretations, when he usually speedily evacuated with farts and explosive noises.

Saddam Hussein and the sadistic stage

A new stage developed in Peter's play when he began to come to me twice a week. His anger and violent war games now became directed against me. He identified with famous dictators and torturers, especially with Saddam Hussein. (It was the time of the Gulf War.) I was supposed to be an American soldier who had to be killed after being brutally tortured. Several times I had to restrain his violent attacks on me. His attacks, both physical and verbal, were always accompanied by a great deal of farting. Whenever he felt like hating me – and in those days it was often – he would say that his foul smell was lethal gas with which he was poisoning me. Sometimes, however, he seemed to be more ambivalent and less full of hate. Then he would warn me that the gas was on the way, and that I should wear a gas mask.

His behavior worsened at times of separation. After each break he would deny having missed me, yet would regularly come back to the sessions with the most vicious plans for revenge against me. He played these out in violent battles or in more subtle torture-chamber games. If I said that he was angry with me because I had been away, he would say that this was not so. Rather he said he wanted to kill me because I was stupid, or for other worse reasons. I interpreted that, because of the break, the "good me" had abandoned him, allowing the "bad me witch" to come out. I said he had had the same feelings as a baby when his mother had left him, and he had felt helpless and tortured in the hospital by the bad doctors. This interpretation moved his games in yet another direction.

The closet game

In my office there is a wall wardrobe with sliding doors. Peter would order me to go into the wardrobe and stay there. I was not to complain or to move. He closed me inside session after session, only occasionally letting me out to sit in my chair. The wardrobe was a spaceship in which he would send me to Mars and then abandon me there. I interpreted that he wanted me to feel like he had felt when I had gone away on my holidays. He was now using the spaceship to send me as far away from him as possible, and from everyone else as well. These feelings, I told him, were the feelings of abandonment he had experienced when I had gone away, just as when he was a baby, he had felt abandoned when his mother had left him.

The reader may recall here that in his early infancy, Peter had been locked in a closet by his mother. I never mentioned this specific episode to him. I chose to work with this significant trauma at the fantasy level in the transference. We know from our analytic work that events of the past are remembered as they were experienced, not as they actually happened, and that memory is not necessarily accurate. Therefore, in the transference we give the patient a chance to communicate by nonverbal projective identification his or her fantastic elaboration of the original experience, and thus attempt to make sense of it. Using reverie and countertransference is the only way available to the analyst to verify a patient's historical data.

In response to my interpretations of his feelings of abandonment, Peter left me on Mars and went back to Earth to fetch some of my friends and relatives so that I would not feel too lonely. However, he told me that he, himself, would not stay on Mars with me. He would fly off with a nice girl who he said was his girlfriend. "It will serve you right for having left me," he said, and in saying this, he seemed to experience a great triumph. I realized that elements of ambivalence were beginning to appear. As much as Peter wanted to punish me, he did not want to make me feel too lonely.

Eventually this game changed and developed into the story of the lost pussycat.

The lost pussycat

Peter told me a story about a little pussycat that had lost its mother. The mother wandered around meowing desperately, searching for her lost baby. In a corner of the room the baby was crying and calling for its mommy, but he could not find her, nor she him. Peter explained how the two cats had become separated and lost from each other. I commented on how hungry and cold and scared the baby cat must feel. He said he would take care of the kitten and provide a warm shelter for it.

My couch is made of two futon mattresses. Peter would become the baby pussycat and curl up on one mattress and ask me to cover him with the other. He would meow incessantly session after session, while I sat next to him, commenting how awful it must be for that poor kitten without its mommy, and with no milk to drink. Peter asked me to give him a bottle. I pretended to give him one, and he pretended to suck vigorously. However, any attempts on my part to link the baby pussycat with the baby Peter were instantly rejected. He would become angry and shout at me, "Stop it, you stupid, it's not me, it's the pussycat!" Worse insults followed if I did not stop immediately.

The pretend feeding game did, however, allow me to witness the pussycat's fits of insatiable hunger. Peter would pretend to devour the pillows, the couch, the chair, the room with me in it, New Mexico, the United States, the whole world, and even outer space. After all this eating, he would become fat, super-fat, and eventually he would explode and everything would come bursting back out of him. I believe this game well illustrated the dynamics of his projectile vomiting as an infant, and his anxiety about deprivation, both physical and emotional. Later on in our play I was ordered to stuff myself with great amounts of food that he would prepare for me. Then I had to pretend to vomit. At this stage in the therapy, he accompanied this game with meowing, farting noises, and actual farts. His farts were especially loud when he was demonstrating how pussycat, after having eaten the whole world, would explode. Usually he had to rush to the toilet so as not to soil his pants.

At this point in my narrative, I would like to make some technical comments. It was clear to me that during the closet game Peter began to exhibit some signs of ambivalence. These could be considered rudimentary feelings of concern for the analyst/mother. This ambivalent state is what Klein calls the depressive position. It occurs when a baby is able to experience both strong destructive and positive affects toward the same object. The surfacing of Peter's positive feelings for me made him feel an overwhelming sense of depressive guilt for the damage he feared he had caused me by hating me. When a patient like Peter reaches this stage, and the ambivalent feelings become too powerful, usually a temporary regression occurs. In this case, Peter regressed to fantasies of persecution and to manic acting out, just as we were beginning to make progress. Jung talks about this temporary regression as occurring in the service of the ego. Peter's regression developed at the beginning of the second year of our work together. The farts and farting noises, in spite of my constantly interpreting their meaning, increased in a manic crescendo. I began to feel impotent, unable to ever break through to him or alter the situation by verbal communication. My words seemed to bounce back at me, transformed into farts. He managed to turn my alpha-element interpretations back into beta-elements (Bion 1988) and then evacuate them back at me, not allowing any processing of material to occur. I felt he had enveloped himself tightly in an invisible barrier of smells and farts that acted as protection against any external communication in the area of his greatest distress. To use Michael Fordham's conceptualization, one could say that the farts were manifestations of defenses of the self, the aim of which was the maintenance of an infantile, perverted state of mind. In my countertransference, I felt powerless and choked by Peter's responses. His attacks seemed aimed at expelling all meaning from my communications, turning everything I said to him into so much hot air. Not only was this defensive autistic barrier of farts preventing communication, it was also keeping his baby self in a state of isolation and abandonment. It was recreating for him the distressing infantile situation of the absent "breast/mother," and I, the mother/analyst, was not permitted to comfort him. In the absence of the breast/mother, it appeared that baby Peter had managed to hold himself together using the smell of his farts and excrement as an autistic object.

Switching roles

In his paper "Countertransference" (1985), Fordham discusses "deviations from the analytic attitude," where analysts have forcefully expressed their affects. Such responses to the patient's transference, Fordham states, are "non-analytic and . . . may be classified as countertransference." He mentions a case quoted by Jung, in which one of Jung's patients threatens to hit him, and Jung responds that if she dares, he will hit her back. Fordham adds:

> [These responses] are usually aggressive and seem to be common with patients who are borderline, have psychotic traits, or are frankly psychotic. Often they take place when the patient threatens the analyst's posture and self-definition, either by consistently acting out or by frustrating the analytic process or by attacking the analytic frame.
>
> (Fordham 1985: 146)

My frustration with Peter became so extreme that – after struggling with my internal analyst who kept advising me to stick to verbal interpretations – I decided to counterattack: I altered my technique and acted out his own games for him, including the making of loud farting noises of my own.

At first, Peter was very much surprised and puzzled by my behavior, not believing that I could act in such a way. I took his surprise and puzzlement as a clue that he was beginning to hear me, and this encouraged me to keep on with my approach. His surprise was soon followed by annoyance, and then anger that I kept making farting noises. He did not want to hear such noises from me; he wanted to be the only one who could make them. He called me crazy and ordered me to stop. When I did not, he screamed insults at me and physically attacked me. After a while he gave me a long, steady look, and then burst out in wholehearted laughter. At this I stopped, and – reverting to my interpretive mode – I told him I had wanted to demonstrate to him what he sounded like. I told him that I had noticed that he used farting to stop communication, as if he wanted to make me believe he was crazy. I said that in the past, he had managed to convince people that he was crazy, and had succeeded in being rejected because of it. The behavior I had just shown him was extremely annoying, and had caused him to be disliked by other children, his teachers, and even his parents. I added that in the sessions he had tried to make me dislike him too, and that when he was a baby and his mommy had left him, he had imagined that his behavior had caused her abandonment. If I left him too, then there would be no-one on the whole planet would could comfort him and love him. He would feel miserable and alone and would have to hold himself together by farting to keep himself from falling into total despair, just as when he was a baby, he had comforted himself by smelling his own warm, familiar body smells.

This rather all-embracing interpretation derived from my countertransference emotions, including the fact that I have an extremely fine olfactory sensitivity, which made me very aware of his smell and very weary. The way I have phrased the interpretation here is a condensation of several short comments and interpretations that I was able to make to Peter as his defenses began to loosen up. It seems to have made sense of Peter's projective identification, for a real change occurred in his behavior. His farting decreased and he allowed himself a closer and warmer relationship with me. The play of space wars and explosions diminished considerably, except at times of regression around breaks. He began to relate to me like a "real" child.

The primal scream

Peter became interested in two soft toys that had been in the box all along, but which he had hardly noticed before. These were a girl rabbit, pretty and dressed in pink, and Garfield-the-Cat, the character from the comic books. Peter sat on a chair opposite me and picked up the two toys. He said that they lived in our respective homes. He hugged and cuddled them and called them his babies. But he quickly became impatient with them because they were crying. He began to beat them and fling them into the air or across from his chair onto mine as if he were throwing them into outer space. I caught the toys in mid-air and cuddled them, saying I was there to protect them. Peter became engrossed in the play. I made the animals cry and complain about the way they were being treated and how frightened they were of falling forever into the void or crashing down and being killed.

Peter began to act out the animals' fear. He said that Garfield-the-Cat was famous for being fearful and that he would show me how Garfield could scream. He then crawled along the floor and suddenly emitted a shrill, terrifying scream. It was a shriek of unspeakable dread. The high pitch penetrated my head and I felt as if it would penetrate my eardrums. The despair in his voice was intolerable. The screaming went on and on – for a good 15 minutes – until Peter was completely breathless. It was truly a "primal scream."

After Peter calmed down, I told him that he had shown me not only Garfield's fear, but also his own: the fear he had experienced as a tiny baby when his mother had left him, when she had taken away all that was safe and familiar to him. He lay on the couch; he did not reject my interpretation. He asked me to tuck him in, and then started to suck his thumb. At the end of the session he was unable to walk out by himself, and his mother had to carry him to the car.

I will stop here in my narrative, although Peter continued to present much interesting material in the course of his treatment. After this session in which he was finally able to break through his primitive form of communication – farting – to his anguished, but human, scream of dread, dramatic changes occurred in his manner of relating to me, and to his parents, teachers, and schoolmates.

Discussion

Important elements that need to be stressed in the case of Peter are the actual facts of his neglect, hospitalization, and maternal abandonment. Experiences of this sort evoke and foster grandiose fantasies and infantile omnipotence as defenses against feelings of helplessness and dread. Such experiences also damage the development of symbolic thinking. Children who are deprived of an emotional container in infancy later on lack any sense of boundaries or the capacity to contain and process their emotions. They have no expectation of continuity in relationships, and often play at falling forever or being dropped. Sometimes these children drop their toys, or perch perilously, jump, or let themselves fall. These actions seem to be concrete enactments of their sense of having been dropped or gotten rid of.

Peter needed our analytic sessions to build the emotional container in which he could work through his primitive feelings. Previously when he was distressed, he used his farts to create a container for his infant self, enveloping himself in his own familiar, comforting smell. The farts were also aggressive. Like a skunk, he both protected himself and attacked his enemies with a barrier of poisonous smell.

The French psychoanalyst Didier Anzieu has developed the idea of "psychic envelopes." Anzieu sees the ego as surrounded by a number of sensory envelopes, the olfactory envelope being one that in his view is

> neither continuous nor solid. It is riddled with a great number of holes, corresponding to the pores of the skin, and which lack controllable sphincters; these holes allow the excess of inner aggressiveness to seep out . . . . This envelope of smells is, moreover, fuzzy, vague and porous; it does not allow for the sensory differentiations which are at the root of the activity of thinking.
>
> (Anzieu 1989: 182)

Anzieu's concept of the envelope of smell as an example of a sensory container was in my mind as I worked with Peter. Smell is one of the most developed senses in infancy. The smell of the mother's milk directs the baby to the breast. It promotes the earliest deintegration of the primary self in support of survival. In Peter's case, the loss of the mother's familiar smell was substituted, in an autistic way, by the smells from his own body. These smells had the function of isolating him, but also of protecting him from external dangers.

We know that early abandonment increases omnipotent fantasies.

In Peter's case we can witness the effect of early disintegrative experiences. To adopt Michael Fordham's conceptualization, we could say that the deintegration of Peter's primary self, instead of occurring in the container of his relationship with his mother, had occurred in "outer space," that is, in an emotional void. The absence of a good-enough maternal element had made Peter unable to metabolize and integrate his distressing primitive experiences. Thus his capacity for symbolic thinking had been impaired, and the imagery activated in his infant psyche remained archetypal and terrifying. However, because of his early experience of the love and care of his adoptive parents, along with his innate resilience, Peter had the potential for building a solid container within the therapeutic encounter.

Interactional field and countertransference

I would now like to describe some of the difficulties that occur in the analyst's countertransference when working with such a child. Peter's case was a major challenge. I constantly had the feeling of being an "absent object" to him, and he made me doubt my own ability to be effective. He did not seem to acknowledge my presence, just as his mother did not acknowledge him in his infancy; I felt ignored, humiliated, and forgotten – again, just as he must have felt. The amount of projective identification I had to process was extreme and very draining on my emotional energy. My response to this lack of acknowledgement was to want to force him to feel my presence. I became more active than I usually am in sessions to the point of frank counterattack. I believe that I needed to bring myself and Peter's infant self back to life and claim the presence of both of us in the world. There were also great difficulties with Peter's parents, whose own psychological needs were too great to allow them to understand his. I had to manage them and their anxieties gently but firmly in order to make the work with Peter possible.

Peter's transference was primitive, chaotic, violent; his play presented many of the characteristics of deprived children described by Mary Boston – endless evacuation and falling (Boston and Szur 1983: 22). His projective identification was massive, and his destructive envy operated to prevent any change and to negate both my efforts and his own potential for recovery.

The game of Garfield-the-Cat allowed Peter finally to break out of his primitive, animal-like mode of communicating. Once this breakthrough had been integrated, he reached a genuinely human form of expressing his dread and despair. Instead of enveloping me with farts, he was able to show me his pain. He let out his love and his tears, and also his acute observations and his sense of humor. I was able to share his feelings of dread, and a space was created between us in which he could allow himself to feel close to me. In time he was able to feel happy and laugh and even joke. After three years of therapy, dramatic changes occurred in all his relationships, and he began to function in a manner appropriate to his age. Still much work needed to be done, but a space in which the work could take place had now been created.

Chapter 6

The shadow

How it develops in childhood

In this chapter I will focus on the archetype of the shadow. In Jungian terms, the shadow is that part of the personality of which one is the least aware and therefore is in the dark about. Similarly, we are unaware of the way in which our body parts function to keep us alive. There are two aspects of the shadow, the personal or oedipal shadow and the collective or pre-oedipal shadow. My hypothesis is that the material that we associate with the *collective shadow* pertains to the psychosomatic realm and is shaped by one's earliest infantile affective experiences. The contents of the *personal shadow* belong mainly to the oedipal stage of development.

In this chapter, using material from two analytic cases, I will illustrate the way in which affective discharges from the beginning of life constellate typical imagery and fantasies that Jung defined as archetypal.

Affects, body, and shadow

The American psychologist Sylvan Tomkins (1962; 1963) identified a system of basic affects, classified in two groups: positive ones such as joy and interest; and negative ones such as distress, fear, anger, disgust, and shame.

Recent research in neurobiology and endocrinology provides evidence that infant persecutory states are exacerbated by emotional deprivation and parental neglect to the extent that development of symbolic thinking is impaired. It has been scientifically demonstrated that violence, abandonment, and emotional deprivation suffered at an early age become etched in the brain and negatively influence behavior. Conversely, a loving and emotionally consistent parental presence reduces persecutory states and fosters healthy emotional growth.

Because of his background in neuropsychiatry, Jung was one of the first analysts to understand the importance of early affects on emotional life. Jung wrote:

> Emotion, incidentally, is not an activity of the individual but something that happens to him. Affects occur usually where adaptation is weakest, and at the same time they reveal the reason for its weakness, namely a certain degree of inferiority and an existence of a lower level of personality.
>
> (Jung 1951b: 8–9)

Early defense mechanisms, the most common of which is splitting, allow the infant to separate bad feelings from good ones. The bad feelings that persecute the infant's ego are pushed out and projected onto the mother/environment, while the good ones are kept inside to aid survival. This is called the schizoid/paranoid system of defenses; when it is set in motion, given the urgency of infantile states, it helps the infant to comfort himself.

I would like at this point to shed light on the body that throws the shadow and to explore the relationship that a body has with its own shadow. Having a body places humans in the physical universe, causing them to suffer and eventually to become aware of the limitations that universal laws impose upon the boundlessness of the imagination. The area of the imaginal is where the "chaotic magma" of the primitive shadow acquires a mental representation that can be owned or can be split off, disowned, and eventually projected as far away as is needed for the subject to feel safe.

Jung brought attention to the transforming power of archetypal processes and stressed the need to integrate shadow contents as the major task of individuation in the second part of life. The process leads to psychosomatic wholeness. Affects have a clearly identifiable physiological response; therefore, they belong to the psychosomatic area and reveal the deep connection between emotions and the body. In fact, affective manifestations are physical representations of internal states, made visible through bodily changes. Jung wrote:

> On the one hand, emotion is the alchemical fire whose warmth brings everything into existence and whose heat burns all superfluities to ashes . . . . But on the other hand, emotion is the moment when steel meets flint and a spark is struck forth, for emotion is the chief source of consciousness. There is no change from darkness to light or from inertia to movement without emotion.
>
> (Jung 1938: 96)

Violent affects in infancy disrupt the process of ego formation; therefore, the ego engages in disposing of (splitting), hiding away (persona), or burying in the body its disturbing emotions which evoke dread of disintegration.

The collective shadow

The contents of the collective shadow are primitive and ruthless and are to be found in all human beings exposed to survival threats. They are related to destructive and evil elements in human nature and are derivatives of the death instinct. They are compounded in every culture by prejudices and preconceived ideas mixed with paranoid elements.

These perverse and murderous elements are life-threatening, and are evoked primarily by survival anxiety. Under normal circumstances they are kept under control, subject to moral condemnation from the adult part of the ego and the superego. In situations of regression the ego weakens and can fall back into being possessed by the shadow archetype's primitive contents. This happens more easily in groups because the group ego is more labile, and masses are more likely to be gripped by paranoid states.

Mythical elaborations of primitive contents derived from archetypal drives provide the physiological substrate for mythical archetypal imagery. For instance, oral sadistic cannibalistic fantasies originate in the course of hungry attacks on the breast/mother in states of uncontrollable hunger, and can be imaginatively represented at the collective level by fierce beasts and divinities which devour their young. Loaded with affects of terror, horror, or excitement, these images come up in dreams and nightmares where images of bloodshed, torture, and death can extend to other sensory modalities and constellate images of dismemberment, bodily explosions, and annihilation. These also merge into collective consciousness, expressed in myths and artistic imagery.

When the contents of the primitive shadow remain unconscious, a person or group can become possessed by the collective shadow archetype and act out wars, murder, and destruction. These shadow contents can also possess the body and be somatized in destructive illnesses such as cancer or immune system collapse, hysterical paralysis, heart failure, and so on, and never reach a mental representation. These contents can also be acted out in psychological perversions.

Whenever this sort of material breaks loose and erupts into consciousness it causes a psychotic breakdown because shadow affective contents overpower ego defense mechanisms. The ego disintegrates and the ego complex is gripped by the shadow.

In infancy, due to the lack of differentiation between psyche and soma, experiences are psychosomatic, that is, essentially affective. They resonate instantly in physiological responses because body and psyche are felt to be one and the same.

According to Jungian developmental theory, archetypal drives activate instinctual bodily needs and bring the infant into relationship with the mother/environment, which promotes consciousness and ego growth.

In my view, the roots of the pre-oedipal (collective) shadow can be traced back and found deeply embedded in instinctual drives and affective responses. Therefore, the contents of the collective shadow are most threatening to psychological stability and must be defended against.

Such drives and responses are located in the body, loaded with affect, and usually discharged in activity. In infancy, when ego and impulse control are weak, these contents feel uncontainable. The infant therefore needs a mother/caregiver to function as an auxiliary ego-consciousness for her infant when he is in states of overwhelming affective pressure. She modifies, contains, and transforms such affects into manageable emotional states so that eventually the child can think about and represent his experience symbolically in words.

However, when these instinctual needs are not met, and the infant ego cannot find a soothing and calming mother, the mother's shadow, which is witch-like and related to destruction, death, and evil, colors the infant's experience. The infant feels persecuted by negative affects such as murderous rage and envy, which he needs to expel and dispose of outside of himself.

While archetypes are experienced in life through archetypal images, archetypal drives need to undergo transformation to be representable in images. The process of transformation from concrete to symbolic, from affective discharges to symbolic thinking, begins in early infancy and needs the mother's transcendent function to be activated in the infant's psyche. Jung defined the transcendent function as a "mediatory product" which

> forms the raw material for a process not of dissolution but of construction, in which both thesis and antithesis play their part. In this way it becomes a new content that governs the whole attitude, putting an end to the division and forcing the energy of the opposites into a common channel. The standstill is overcome and life can

flow on with renewed power towards new goals. I have called this
process in its totality the *transcendent function* . . . .

(Jung 1921: 480)

Therefore, we can say that the transcendent function exists as a predisposition, dormant in the infant psyche, which develops over time,
given the right kind of nurturing. An infant who feels persecuted is difficult to hold, soothe, and comfort; he represents a challenge to a mother
who may feel ill-equipped to cope with her infant's distress and
dramatic neediness. When she is unable to cope, she experiences the
infant as "bad." Unable to transform the infant's distressed state, the
mother feels helpless and blames the infant for her shortcomings. Thus,
the infant's affects remain unmodified and untransformed, and are negatively reinforced by the mother's negative projections. In this way a
distressed infant who *feels* bad *becomes* bad in his mother's eyes and
cannot receive solace for his unspeakable distress. Moreover, the infant
experiences the mother as the "killer witch," and a vicious cycle of pain,
rage, frustration, and fear sets in. An infant is unable to differentiate
between his contribution and the contribution of the environment to his
catastrophic feelings, so he feels that the mother/world is to blame for all
the atrocities of illness, terror, and pain that he feels in the moment and
imagines he will have to endure forever.

In these cases, the distressed infant experiences the mother as the
wicked witch of fairy tales, and, in turn, the infant becomes to the frustrated mother a devouring monster.

When the experience of dependency turns negative it evokes survival
panic, anxiety, frustration, rage, and murderous feelings. Frustration
generated by this state of affairs is made more tolerable for the baby by
omnipotent archetypal fantasies of self-fulfillment created by halluci-
nating the "good mother" archetype, and/or by splitting defenses.

Fordham writes about this phenomenon: "That the archetypes form
the basis of psychic life in childhood . . . can no longer be doubted, yet,
because the ego is weak, their activity is liable to result in many critical
anxieties" (Fordham 1973: 101).

An infant using the defense mechanisms that Fordham called
"defenses of the self" can protect himself from affective states and feelings that threaten survival of the self. Fordham stated that the primary
self is equipped with defense mechanisms that in a situation of extreme
danger keep the infant isolated in the world of archetypal fantasies.

The personal shadow

In contrast to the collective shadow, the personal shadow is formed in response to distressing experiences the child's ego feels in the process of growing up. These contents are mainly oedipal senses of shame and inferiority. In the course of the process of adaptation, which occurs in the first part of life, a person requires a directed conscious ego function characterized by inner consistency and logical coherence. Because the conscious function is directed, everything unsuitable must be excluded to maintain the integrity of direction. The unsuitable elements are subjected to inhibition and thereby escape attention; they slowly contribute to form the stuff the personal shadow is made of. That is the part of oneself that one hates, which is disowned by the ego and belongs to a later stage of development. Apropos of this, Jung wrote:

> [The contents of the shadow] are not only of an infantile-sexual character, but are altogether incompatible contents and tendencies, partly immoral, partly unaesthetic, partly again of an irrational, imaginary nature. The obviously inferior character of these contents as regards adaptation has given rise to [a] depreciatory view of the psychic background . . . . What the regression brings to the surface certainly seems at first sight to be slime from the depths; but if one does not stop short at a superficial evaluation . . . this "slime" contains not merely incompatible and rejected remnants of everyday life, or inconvenient and objectionable animal tendencies, but also germs of new life and vital possibilities for the future.
>
> (Jung 1928: 34–5)

Thus the personal shadow appears to contain a mixture of negative and positive attributes of the self which were disowned and cast away in childhood because they were unappreciated and condemned by the collective in which the person has grown up. Like sunken treasures, these contents need rescuing from the bottom of the sea of the unconscious.

My hypothesis is that in childhood the ego adopts defense mechanisms to protect itself from those contents that Jung defined as "animal tendencies" within us that would constitute an "unpleasant discovery" and threaten ego stability, which is especially required in latency. A sternly rigid upbringing can contribute to a person's hiding his or her emotions and disposing of valuable personal attributes into the personal shadow, which grows and thrives at the expense of consciousness.

This aspect of the shadow is usually more accessible because it is closer to consciousness. Even so, it requires considerable struggle to access the personal shadow, since it contains unpleasant aspects and truths about us. We become aware of these aspects of ourselves at a later stage of development when a sense of concern for the object has begun to develop. Becoming aware of the shadow makes one feel as if one is a "bad guy" and is related to the stage of development that Melanie Klein called the depressive position, when the child feels guilt and remorse for his bad behavior towards his love objects.

The personal shadow's contents are mostly oedipal, centering around power, gender issues, and control connected to the reality of the help-lessness and inadequacy of a young child who needs to survive with the help of a caring parent and yet resents it. The emotions of love and hate for the parental objects are intense and in conflict. There is ambivalence toward the object, and moods shift quickly. The young child feels the need to repress the violence of his emotions, which generate strong anxiety in him. In the personal shadow, both of older children and of adults in therapy, one finds "germs of new life and vital possibilities for the future." These often are positive aspects of the personality, for the most part healthy aggressive impulses. They had to be suppressed in early childhood when the child lacked the capacity to regulate the force of his emotions and the parents were punitive and repressive instead of helping the child to regulate them.

The personal shadow, which is represented as the repressed uncon-scious, is a depository of all the stuff that the child's ego is unable to deal with or take responsibility for without feelings of ambivalence or conflict. Through repression these elements are prevented from coming into relation with the conscious parts of the ego. As splitting and evacuation are the defense mechanisms for early shadow material, so repression is the defense that makes the shadow grow during latency.

The aggressive elements and fantasies generated by the oedipal con-flict are compounded by powerful emotions of love and hate, pleasure and fear, stirred by the stirrings of genital identity and development. These are at the root of the personal shadow during latency when instinctual material is heavily repressed.

Such mechanisms are reinforced in collective structures and social institutions as an effective means of controlling a group. Political, religious, military, and professional organizations tend to operate in this way. In the same way that an infant splits his object in order to do away with its frustrating elements, which are equated with badness, so a group can split its unwanted parts instead of processing them.

The shadow in analysis

All analysts recognize how hard it is for patients to work with their shadow as present and real in the transference–countertransference dynamics of the analytic session. The process of assimilating the shadow presents a moral dilemma. Jung wrote: "The shadow is a moral problem that challenges the whole ego-personality, for no one can becomes conscious of the shadow without considerable moral effort" (Jung 1951b: 8).

In spite of efforts toward integration, the shadow can never be fully assimilated. Through analysis one begins to own the personal shadow and to become aware of the limitations of his or her nature. Also through analysis one may begin to come to terms with aspects of the pre-oedipal shadow, as it may be represented by somatization, and unregulated primitive affects.

John

This patient struggled with pre-oedipal shadow contents that were manifested in all sorts of physical pains and symptoms. John presented an overdetermined identification with a rigid persona, which he referred to as "the feeling of wearing a mask." This served to give him the illusion of disguising the most infantile, primitive, and undifferentiated part of himself – the pre-oedipal part of his distressed life shadow. John had dealt with his unbearable feelings by splitting and dissociating from them.

Discussing this state of affairs, Jung wrote:

> Such dissociations came about because of various incompatibilities; for instance, a man's present state may have come into conflict with his childhood state . . . . He has thus become unchildlike and artificial, and has lost his roots. [T]his presents a favourable opportunity for an equally vehement confrontation with the primary truth.
>
> (Jung 1951a: 162)

Fordham (1973) developed this statement further: "How important is the shadow of maturity, i.e., infantilism, in arriving at a wholeness which is the aim of individuation" (p. 96). He goes on to say:

> constant interaction between the maturing psychic organism and the environment is what produces development. If the infant's varying

needs are not sufficiently met, it is known that maturation is retarded or stopped, and false solutions are arrived at, which later on cannot be used to meet the "tasks of life" demanded of an adult . . . .
(Fordham 1973: 98)

When John referred himself to the clinic, he was in his late twenties. He was a social worker in charge of a children's home. He looked much younger than his age, was of medium height and very skinny and wiry. He projected the image of fragmentation, like a collage of mismatched bits that I felt reflected his inner emotional state. He appeared very emotionally immature.

Although he had asked for therapy, he felt the only ones in need of looking after were the children in his care. He had difficulty acknowledging that he might have some needs too. He couldn't take any time away from the children and looked after them with total dedication, day and night.

His account of his life depicted an unhappy childhood both at home and at school. Throughout it all there were lengthy descriptions of illness and solitary play. He had had a difficult start in life; he was the second of three born to a young, inexperienced mother who herself had suffered maternal deprivation, having been brought up in a children's home. She never physically abused her children; her violence was acted out in fights with her husband.

After a difficult breech delivery, John was separated from his mother for two weeks, for she had developed a serious postpartum complication. Thus he suffered at birth a long separation from his mother, which had great implications for his troubles in later life. As an infant he was left to his own resources in the grip of survival panic, which he still experienced during times of uncertainty.

The mother and baby John never seemed to work out a good emotional fit. They shared the omnipotent fantasy of having damaged each other, which tainted their relationship, making it unsuccessful. This of course meant that John had experienced the negative side of dependency, which would have to be worked out in the transference and countertransference of analysis.

John's father suffered from nervous breakdowns and depressions. He was prone to fits of temper and used to hit John for no apparent reason. The parents quarreled frequently and violently, which frightened John. At seventeen, John became involved with drugs, sought treatment, and eventually studied to become a social worker.

John complained of unsatisfactory relationships with both men and women whom, it emerged, he both idealized and despised. After the breakdown of a love affair, he developed violent panic attacks, which paralyzed him and interfered with both his work and his private life.

Through the years, he suffered from a variety of physical symptoms of a psychosomatic sort – pains in his legs and stomach, headaches, dizziness, anorexia, and a total inability to relax. He smoked heavily and in adolescence had been addicted to drugs. During his panic attacks he felt sure he would fade away and die.

In my view, the psychosomatic symptoms pointed to early trauma related to the abandonment, panic, and dread he had actually experienced as an infant separated from his mother. In order to survive, baby John had split off the agony of fear and pain into his body, which became the carrier/container of the persecutory stuff that was trying to kill him. His mother could not help him make sense of his distress because of her own deficit in this area. Thus the lack of the maternal transformative regulation of the baby's emotions continued until he came to analysis.

At the beginning, John was often breathless, tense, and in an almost constant state of fear. Through half-closed eyes he kept scanning the room and me. He talked constantly both to keep me at a distance and to placate me, for he expected that I wanted him to talk. Although his body revealed his state of panic, he related his past painful and disturbing experiences in a monotonous and unemotional tone. I suggested that he lie on the couch. After overcoming considerable anxieties, he did so, seeming to comply out of fear. He kept his body stiff and looked as if he were ready to spring up and run away.

John's account of his early life and childhood consisted of a list of victimizations he had suffered from his parents and at school. He always felt inferior and in danger. He seemed unable to recall warm and happy moments in the family or at school. He mainly recalled his parents' constant and violent quarrels.

Thus it was difficult for John to access his own shadow parts for he felt exclusively the victim of abuse and persecution. He was in total denial of his own destructiveness, which he acted out and projected onto other people, causing them to dislike him. This situation was immediately projected into the transference.

He reported two dreams in the first interview. The first was about a latency-age child being sent to the moon, where he feels very frightened and lonely. He goes into a telephone booth and desperately tries to call earth. The second dream is about himself going to the dentist and being terrified; he fears he will be drugged and die. This dream relates to his anxiety of beginning analysis.

My countertransference soon alerted me to the kind of difficulties we would encounter in the course of the analysis, the degree of his pathology, and the intensity of his transference to me as the witch/ persecutor/dentist.

Children emotionally deprived in infancy live in archetypal fantasy worlds. Without an adult to help them make sense of their experience, they identify with the darkest parts of the collective shadow and their experiences do not become humanized. Their emotions remain unregulated and their impulses uncontrollable.

These children seem to have to experience living "beyond the unpleasure principle" (Alvarez 1992). They identify with rejects, with the shadow of humans. In order to be acceptable, they need more than ordinary children to disguise their shadow. John did this by using his "good social worker" persona as a mask to cover up his horrific inner situation, which he had split off as a child and had been unable to process on his own.

In our work, John often felt I was messing him up with my interpretations and my schedule's restrictions, which he hated. His hatred for me was violent and tangible. He could just barely contain his impulse to hit me.

As his analyst I had to endure being ignored, despised, hated, omnipotently disposed of as a reject, and filled up with garbage. I had to accept his massive projective identifications, make sense of them, and think about them while holding the situation in space and time. I had to survive his merciless attacks on my existence, my feelings, and my own retaliatory murderous wishes towards him.

I had to be very much in tune with him to pick up the slightest signals coming from his body posture, facial expression, and so on, and to make sense of them for myself. I observed that my presence and my facial expression were more important to him than my actual words. I also observed that the tone of my voice, the degree of light in the room, the temperature, and all kinds of other minute details could have a dramatic effect upon him.

His dreams contained many primitive psychotic images: cannibals, dismembered body parts, vampires, cemeteries where the dead and ghosts came out of tombs. He often dreamed of himself as a corpse in a sepulchre.

His fear of devouring or violently damaging me, as he felt he had done to his mother in his infancy, kept him away from sessions, as he had to hide his destructive feelings. No wonder that John had adopted the mask of the good child and of the benefactor of lost children.

The analysis broke down after seventeen months of difficult work, as a result of his tremendous conflicts about returning to treatment after each break or holiday. In his primitive emotional state, whenever he felt abandoned or frustrated, he had a compulsive need to act out a ruthless revenge against me, the mother/analyst who had become the archetypal witch.

Michael

Michael is another patient whose early problems with his mother left him imprisoned in the mother complex, identified with the eternal child, and unable to access shadow contents of aggression, hate, and rage.

In his early seventies, Michael was referred to me by a colleague who had seen him and his wife in couple therapy. She advised him that he needed individual work to understand his difficulties with his wife.

Michael presented himself as youthful and friendly. He appeared very fit and had an innocent-looking face in spite of his mature age, like a little boy who never grew up. I found his childlike expression charming. He was a former minister who had worked on campus, and I imagined that his innocent appearance had inspired trust. Since his retirement he had worked as a pastoral counselor in private practice.

His problem, he immediately told me, was his relationship with his wife. He described her as a temperamental woman, prone to violent rages. Her behavior was frightening and incomprehensible since he could not see the connection between her rages and his own behavior, which she said caused them. He complained that on several occasions she had totally lost control and had physically attacked him. He reported these dramatic events in an affectless, sweet, slightly condescending way, as if reporting a child's bad behavior to a parent. Although he complained, he did not seem to expect any possibility of change. He seemed not to have any problem of his own; his wife was his problem.

When I suggested that I could only work with his personal problems, he sounded resigned and then added meekly that he could not carry on like this any longer. He could not sleep at night and had heart problems every time his wife ill-treated him. He was worried for his heart, even though a heart specialist had reassured him that his heart was fine and that the symptoms were psychosomatic, due to stress. He did not know what to do. He did not want to leave her and yet he feared she would kill him by provoking a heart attack.

My attempts to make him focus on himself failed; each time he reverted to speaking about the way his wife's behavior affected him. His defense system seemed impregnable.

He said he was paralyzed by her attacks and that his only option was to appease her in every possible way. However, this made her even more angry. It sounded as if she wanted to draw him out into an open battle, but he would not let her. He reported feeling totally under her control because if he did not please her, she would not love him and would leave him, as his first wife had done. He complained that she rejected him whenever he wanted to make love. She accused him of not liking her body and of being in love with beautiful younger women like his students and patients. He repeated again and again that it was not true and that he loved only her, but to no avail. Her refusal to make love frustrated and humiliated him.

After several weeks of his reiterating how much he was in love with his wife in spite of all the tortures she inflicted on him, I said it was difficult to understand why he loved her so much while she treated him so badly. Perhaps, I said, there was a part of him that at some level enjoyed being tortured. Maybe was repeating with his wife a pattern of his childhood, of his relationship with his mother. I said he was doing the same with me for he appeared to be fearful of what I might do to him if he let my words get inside him.

He did not respond to my interpretation but petulantly kept asking me what he should do. Should he leave her or not? Could she change? What could he do to improve her? He said there seemed to be two persons inside his wife, that she had a side that was very lovely and at times made him very happy.

His complaints and questions filled session after session. Whenever I attempted to shift the focus to him and the part he played in the relationship, he reverted almost automatically to his wife's wrath and his own innocence and anxiety about it. He complained that I was not helping him make up his mind and that I was siding with his wife.

I began to experience frustration in the countertransference, also helplessness and rage. At first I was unaware of the intensity of my countertransferential wrathful feelings, but I caught myself spacing out and being bored with his endless repetitions and extreme passivity. Slowly, however, I became aware of the sort of projective identification that was taking place.

I could then get in touch with his infantile part, still encapsulated in a negative mother complex, which he projected onto his wife and onto me, in an attempt to make us both become the bad mother of his childhood.

Another advantage of his unconscious identification with the internal child was that he could avoid worry of dying in an age-appropriate way; he could be killed only by a heart attack caused by his bad wife.

In Jungian terms he appeared caught up in the *puer* archetype, identified with a particular aspect of the child archetype – the divine child and its enmeshment in the mother complex.

In her book *The Problem of the Puer Aeternus*, Marie-Louise von Franz defines the divine child archetypal motif:

> *Puer Aeternus* is the name of a god of the antiquity. The words themselves come from Ovid's *Metamorphoses* and are there applied to the child-god in the Eleusinian mysteries. Ovid speaks of the child-god Iacchus, addressing him as *Puer Aeternus* and praising him in his role in these mysteries. He is the divine youth who is born in the night in this typical mother-cult mystery of Eleusis and who is a kind of redeemer. He is a god of vegetation and resurrection, the god of divine youth, corresponding to such oriental gods as Tammuz, Attis, and Adonis. The title *puer aeternus* therefore means eternal youth, but we also use it sometimes to indicate a certain type of young man who has an outstanding mother complex . . . . In general, the man who is identified with the archetype of the *puer aeternus* remains too long in adolescent psychology . . . .
>
> (von Franz 1970: 1)

The mother complex

Michael described his relationship to his mother as a child, how he had always felt himself the innocent victim of her moods. He experienced her as bossy, short-tempered, and yet sometimes caring. He said she loved him because he was a well-behaved, bright little boy. There was no room for him to express unhappy or angry feelings. His mother was very possessive of him, the middle son, for she considered him her "special son." She had great expectations of him and tried always to control him.

Fortunately for him, they lived on a farm and he could get away, hiding in the fields, where he took refuge in his imagination. He found peace playing on his own in the yard with the animals and growing his own plants. He also spent time secretly digging a tunnel that he was sure would enable him to escape to China, where he would be left alone. It was easier to imagine escape than to feel bad feelings against his mother because he wanted her to love him and feared abandonment. The few times he had dared to challenge her, she had reported him to his father, who had belted him when he came home from work. Michael described his father as an unhappy man who had failed in his career and was despised by his wife.

On the whole the childhood atmosphere was somber, full of fear and depression. Fun, joy, and happy moments were absent. After his father's bankruptcy they had to live with his maternal grandparents, who despised his father. They did not seem to like the children either but were hospitable because they were "good Christians." He did not mention his two siblings. The Great Depression had ruined his family finances and contributed to his father's depressive illness and his mother's physical illnesses and sadness. Given this family situation, Michael had tried his best to be a good boy, both to make his mother happy since his father was a failure, and also because he feared losing her affection, or worse causing her death. Thus he retreated into his studies or into his imagination and escaped to fantastic places where he could find peace, but he remained very lonely.

In the sessions, I often felt he was talking about his childhood both to please me, for he knew of my interest in children, and to distance me, for fear that I might hurt him or that he might damage me. Another factor that strengthened his resistance seemed to be his terror of moving on, growing old, dying, or staying in therapy forever, which meant becoming trapped by me, the mother/witch.

Thus his defensive technique consisted in castrating my analytic insights and comments. He controlled the sessions in a monotonous refrain. Since he would agree to come only once a week, it was harder to penetrate his defenses. Whenever I attempted an interpretation linking his present behavior to the past, expressing the view that he was no longer a little boy who had to obey and be passive, he agreed with me. But, he would immediately add, he needed me to advise him about what to do. I felt increasingly as if I was hitting a brick wall, and my internal frustration mounted. His surface softness and kindness covered an impenetrable defensive shield. I had the fantasy of him as a child putting his fingers in his ears so as not to hear my comments, which he experienced as parental reproaches.

On the other hand, I thought that he projected his deafness onto me because he was like a broken record, repeating the same complaints as if unheard. I became for him a heartless, unempathic mother/analyst/wife. He confirmed that his wife misunderstood him most of the time.

Four months into the analysis, through my countertransference, I had collected enough evidence of his internal child's murderous rage against

his mother, his mother/wife, and the mother/analyst. I interpreted to him
that he was feeling enraged with his wife and really wanted to kill her,
but could not let himself think about it for fear of actually doing it, just
as he had felt as a child in response to his mother's abuse. His denial was
vehement, so I added that he was now also enraged with me for having
upset him with the interpretation.

He left rather abruptly and the next session brought the following
dream, which had frightened him.

> I receive a phone call from a friend of mine who is a hunter in which
> he tells me he needs me to do him a favor. He has killed a mother
> deer, and her baby fawn is alone and frightened. Since my friend
> cannot go back there, I am to go into the reservation, dispose of the
> mother deer's body, and take care of the baby. I don't want to go,
> but my friend insists, so I agree so as not to upset him. There is a
> gate leading to the park; as I reach it I see a huge male lion standing
> on top of it. I feel paralyzed by fear and as the lion roars I run away.

He was still shaken reporting the dream and did not seem to have any
idea of what it was all about. I commented that the dream seemed to be
an answer to my interpretation in the previous session about his unconscious wish to kill his "dear mother." In the dream, the hunter friend
stands for an aggressive part of himself who is appointed to do the dirty
job. The hunter calls Michael to the scene of the crime to witness
the event, dispose of the dead body, and take care of the abandoned
fawn part of himself who is now motherless because the bad hunter has
killed her.

I suggested that I could also be the friend who precipitated the dream
by interpreting his unconscious murderous rage.

Although he seemed bewildered by the dream and unable to associate
to its contents, the lion had definitely stirred up his curiosity. I found the
dream very important in that it brought forth a compensating symbol
from the unconscious. While Michael's ego felt helpless and impotent,
the roaring lion pointed to an element of masculine potency previously
unavailable to him while he was identified with the frightened child.

Once the image became conscious and his defensive barrier worked
through in subsequent sessions, he eventually became able to take
possession of his own masculine power and feel in charge. This working
through required many sessions, for he continued to return to his litany
of his wife's abuses. Now, however, I could use the image from the
dream to bring his strength to consciousness. I reminded him that he had

met the lion inside him and that our task was to help him use the internal lion's power to make him stronger.
Jung writes:

> Since the unknowable substance of the Mind, i.e., of the unconscious, always represents itself to consciousness in the form of symbols – the self being one such symbol – the symbol functions as a "means of attaining the Other Shore," in other words, as a means of transformation. In my essay on psychic energy I said that the symbol acts as a transformer of energy.
>
> (Jung 1954: 130–1)

It took at least six months of ups and downs on the theme of the lion dream for Michael to begin to make use of the inner lion's potency in his outer life. Alongside this theme his fear of death also began to surface and could be worked on analytically. His heart problem improved. Finally, one day he came in feeling quite assertive and told me that the previous day his internal lion had roared at his wife. He had succeeded in making her shut up, and she had not hit him, nor had he felt he needed to hit her. He felt pleased with himself and empowered. He said that he had always feared feeling hatred because he wanted only to love people.

Now he understood that he needed to let himself feel hatred and rage whenever he felt abused, and that this had given him the strength to roar. We both felt this was a very important step in his therapy, and from this moment began working on termination. He felt he had gotten what he needed from the therapy. I felt he had made an achievement in assimilating the content of the dream and becoming more open to the integrative action of the self.

When he first came to me, his resistance and rigid defenses had interfered with the function of the ego/self axis. His ego, gripped by the fear of acting out his murderous rage, had imprisoned him in his head, splitting off the instinctual part that he experienced as dangerous. This he had projected onto his wife, who automatically acted it out. Only by analyzing my countertransference was I able to make sense of his defenses and to link up the present with the past where the problem had originated.

However, I did not want him to terminate until he had also shown his assertiveness and power to me. One day he came in with great resolve and told me he had decided to terminate in three weeks because it was time to stop and he meant it. He challenged me for the first time in a way that made me feel he was now ready to end.

His ending dreams were positive, showing that his ego/self axis was working more syntonically. The last session he told me he believed our work had been good. He felt it was enough for the time being, but his wife was concerned, feeling it unwise to stop. I said I too felt the work was not finished. He said he knew it but that he could hate now as well as love and that he trusted he could manage. He had made plans for his wife and him to travel to China, the place he had wanted to visit since childhood to get away from his mother. I suggested that he might want to get away from me in the same way, but he said no. He knew he could come back if necessary. Besides, he was taking his wife with him, which meant that he really did not want to escape.

Chapter 7

The psychosoma and the archetypal field

In this chapter I will explore the process by which an individual self, unfolding after birth within the relationship with the maternal object and the cultural matrix, "creates" its internal and external world. I will borrow from Jung's theory of the self and the archetypes and from Michael Fordham's contributions on child analysis and on the self in infancy.

When Michael Fordham felt the need to apply Jung's theory of the psyche to the onset of life, he expanded the scope of analytical psychology and connected it to modern developments in psychoanalysis and infant research.

Alan Schore's 1994 research in the field of neurobiology, regarding affect modulation and the origin of the self, are parallel to archetypal affective states investigated in 1952 by Jung in his paper on synchronicity. At that time Jung was fascinated by Pauli's research in the field of physics. Jung writes:

> The archetypes are formal factors responsible for the organization of unconscious psychic processes: they are "patterns of behaviour." At the same time they have a "specific charge" and develop numinous effects which express themselves as *affects*. The affect produces a partial *abaissement du niveau mental*, for although it raises a particular content to a supernormal degree of luminosity, it does so by withdrawing so much energy from other possible contents of consciousness that they become darkened and eventually unconscious.
>
> (Jung 1952: 436)

However, in an earlier paper titled "On the Nature of the Psyche" written in 1947, Jung discusses at length the connection between and inseparability of physiological and psychological elements as two aspects of the human being which constitute the totality of the self. The dynamic tension between these two poles, mediated by ego consciousness, activates development and change. Although his theory of psychic energy may be revised today, his discovery of archetypal forces at work in the psyche – similar to other forces at work in the wider universe – was an incredible intuitive leap ahead of his time.

Jung's statement that the archetypes express themselves as affects makes sense both from observing an infant's behavior and from working with primitive material in the analysis of regressed adult patients.

However, as analysts we know that when we enter the archetypal field projected by a regressed patient, we need all our skills to navigate through the gales and bring the patient safely ashore. The one-sidedness and/or absoluteness of the patient's affect can disorient the analyst's ego. The archetypal affects operate as attractors in the emotional field similar to the gravitational force in the universe. Gravitational force cannot be superseded without exiting the atmosphere; using this metaphor we can say that archetypal forces can be overcome only by exiting the atmosphere of a specific complex.

One encounters extremely intense affective fields when dealing with very young infants. Typical infant affective responses present that extreme all-or-none quality which Jung ascribes to archetypal states. However, in the case of the infant this situation is due to a developmental deficit in the infantile ego, whose function needs to be shaped and modulated by interaction with the maternal ego consciousness.

Nothing is more forceful than an infant's distressed cry. Similarly, when an archetypal force is at work, the energetic attraction of the complex draws and imprisons all the energy away from the rest of the personality.

In the analytic situation, the complex eventually creates an energetic field that tends also to attract the analyst and risks drawing him or her into its spirals. This is why Jung made it clear that the analyst must have worked through his or her own complexes to be able to resist the attractor in the affective field.

Instinctual discharges and archetypal images

Archetypes are structures not characterized by consciousness which, by interaction with the environment, contribute to the formation of typical imagery. That is, they provide the sensorial experience with its equivalent mental representation.

Whenever instinctual discharges arouse an affect in the individual, they are instantly experienced in the body as urges needing satisfaction. To delay satisfaction requires a certain degree of ego development which is not available to an infant but which can be acquired by constant interaction with the mother/environment and with the acquisition of the sense of time and space.

The compulsive quality of instinctual drives is related to survival needs and is at its strongest in early infancy when ego-functioning is weak.

The emergence of consciousness and ego-structuring takes place within the nursing couple's activities, supported by maternal care during deintegrative–reintegrative sequences during which the infant introjects experiences and assimilates them emotionally, physically, and mentally. The importance of a "good enough" mother can never be stressed enough at this stage of life. Lack of age-appropriate maternal containment can cause disturbances in an individual because early affects were not metabolized and transformed. At the onset of life, neurophysiological drives and discharges prevail. The quality of an infant's experience is totally archetypal; an infant's instinctual needs have a special overwhelming urgency which is expressed by fits of screaming, panic, and other affect-loaded somatizations. Such experiences produce disturbed bodily states since infants have no symbolic language. When the mother is not available to provide words to make sense of the experiences, they remain mute and locked in bodily symptoms.

According to Jung, bodily experiences relating to instinctual discharges constitute the most deeply unconscious psychic elements, which can never become completely conscious. However, a mother who is attuned to her infant's preverbal states can help her infant tolerate them and can give them a name. At the instinctual level where unconsciousness prevails, the somatic reaction is generally automatic and inflexible, and has that all-or-none quality which in extreme cases can even lead to the death of the individual.

All archetypes evoke positive and/or negative affects which in turn have a life-enhancing or a life-destroying potential. Jung stated that the archetype in itself is not knowable, but that it manifests itself in typical imagery with archetypal characteristics and/or in affects that seize the personality.

The primary self and infant development

Michael Fordham applied Jung's theoretical concepts to infancy. From Jung's concept of the self, Fordham derived the "primary self," which in his view represents the totality of the psyche and soma in a germinal state. The primary self is conceptualized as a blueprint, a "steady state of integration" from which psychic and physiological growth will unfold through a dynamic process that Fordham termed "deintegration–reintegration."

Following infant researches, we can postulate in the infant mind the existence of proto-images such as shapes and patterns which will eventually develop into mental representations of experiences that will feed fantasies, dreams, and language when given meaning and processed by a maternal or parental mind. Fordham postulates the primary self as a steady state which must deintegrate in order to allow for the dynamic systems to begin to work.

The psychic energy bound up in the primary integrate divides into opposites, constellating the opposing archetypal experiences, psychophysiological in nature:

1. Positive experiences lead to good, satisfactory, loving, and comforting feelings, thus constellating the good mother archetype.
2. Negative experiences, such as feelings of discomfort, hate, despair, rage, violence, persecution, fear, and panic (during which both mother and infant are experienced by the latter as destroyed) constellate the bad mother archetype.

According to Fordham's theory it follows that archetypal drives shape early experiences. This is in accordance with Jung's view, that "Where instinct predominates, *psychoid* processes set in which pertain to the sphere of the unconscious as elements incapable of consciousness" (Jung 1947: 183–4). However, he further states, "In the psychic sphere, the compulsive pattern of behaviour gives way to variations of behaviour which are conditioned by experience and by volitional acts, that is, by conscious processes" (Jung 1947: 188). In this passage Jung is defining the limits of the potential for consciousness.

Similarly, the British psychoanalyst Bion formulated a theory in which he described the impossibility of some aspects of experience ever reaching consciousness. He said these were somatic in essence, which he called beta elements.

The dyad

In early development the importance of primary maternal care and pre-occupation is self-evident. In the course of infant observation seminars one witnesses the degree of empathy required of a mother to facilitate her infant's difficult life task and can observe how easily an infant can be gripped by terrifying emotional states.

That is to say, the infant can become possessed by aspects of the mother archetype which can be humanized only by the real mother's caring interventions. Thanks to repeated interactions with the real mother, a healthy infant gradually will be able to tolerate the frustration of maternal failures and his own failures, and let go of the need for a perfect fit derived from the archetypal expectation originating from the great mother archetype.

Some infants, however, are born with an extreme sensitivity which makes their task of adapting to life's disturbing stimuli excruciatingly difficult and which is a predictor of a pathological outcome.

Absoluteness is an attribute of the self that is much stressed by Jung. In the case of infants it proves that the self in infancy is active and pre-dominates over the ego. Given the absoluteness of affects, unless the experience is processed and contained by the mother, it is unthinkable and therefore cannot be processed by the infant.

A perfect example of this state of affairs is found in Daniel Stern's *Diary of a Baby*. Stern attempts to enter the psyche of a six-week-old baby and lend him words to describe his experiences in a fit of hunger. Fordham would describe the event as a deintegrative–reintegrative sequence at the onset of a disintegration due to a fit of hunger. Stern writes in a chapter titled "A Hunger Storm":

> It is four hours since Joey's last feeding, and he is probably hungry. Suddenly his lower lip protrudes. He starts to fret. Soon the fretting gives way to jerky crying, then moves into a full cry.
>
> A storm threatens. The light turns metallic. The march of clouds across the sky breaks apart. Pieces of sky fly off in different directions. The wind picks up force, in silence. There are rushing sounds, but no motion. The wind and its sound have separated. Each chases after its lost partner in fits and starts. The world is disintegrating. Something is about to happen.
>
> Uneasiness grows. It spreads from the center and turns into pain.
>
> It is at the center that the storm breaks out. It is at the very center

that it grows stronger and turns into pulsing waves. These waves push the pain out, then pull it back again.

The wind and the sound and the pieces of the sky are all pulled back into the center. There they find one another again, are reunited. Only to be thrown outward and away, then sucked back in to form the next wave – darker and stronger.

The pulsing waves swell to dominate the whole weatherscape. The world is howling. Everything explodes and is blown out and then collapses and rushes back toward a knot of agony that cannot last – but does.

(Stern 1990: 31–2)

Here Stern describes in poetic metaphor that the whole world feels disjointed and fractured in the infant's overwhelming affective state. For Joey, the world is disintegrating. This reflects a profound disruption of his going-on-being. In such a situation the baby enters upon the huge task of making sense of different parts of the world while being in a fractured state. This is why the presence of the good-enough mother is absolutely necessary to weather the storm and bring back a peaceful state of being. By satisfying the infant's violent instinctual urge she produces in the infant a state of total well-being.

Then the world is peaceful, all is calm. Oceanic feelings of being at one with a beautiful, calm, loving world can give rise to a sense of harmony, beauty, and joy. These feelings are also archetypally determined and are attributed to the good mother archetype.

Repetitions of both kinds of experience, modulated by the actual mother's interventions, contribute to build up the infant's sense of himself and to make sense of the world outside. In this way the infant begins to differentiate the experience of reality from the experience of the archetypal realm. In non-pathological circumstances the archetypal experiences recede as they become incarnated in human experiences. The world of fantasy becomes differentiated from the external world of reality. The infant begins to exist in space and time.

Thus the affects become regulated and transformed by the mother's reverie. The archetypal energy released during the infant's deintegrative phase is transformed and diffused and becomes available for symbolic play and thinking.

An example of an infant observed

Sheila is a baby who does not cry when in distress but tries desperately to contain and control herself in a do-it-yourself kind of modality. Her self-regulatory function is impaired and distorted because of her mother's inability to function as an external regulator for her baby. Sheila tries to do away with expectations of help from her mother. Sheila's mother is poorly attuned to her baby. This is clearly observable from the infant observation tape. The videotape was recorded at a dramatic time when Sheila had just returned home from a week in the hospital for a severe urinary tract (urethral reflux) infection. Apart from tension displayed in muscular activity and a distressed look in her eyes, there is no open demand on her part to be cuddled, comforted, or held in arms. She seems resigned to cope with distress on her own.

From the start, attachment to the mother had been fraught with rejection and ambivalence on the mother's part, so that the father had stepped in, stopping work after Sheila's birth, to take over her care. However, after two months he had to return to work, and the baby developed severe somatic symptoms which we assumed were due to the loss of his care which, although less than optimal, had been the best available.

The tape shows Sheila struggling on her own with the bottle to the utmost of her possibilities. She does not cry for help even though her parents are around. It is a very interesting example of how, in the case of poor attachment, a child feels that she has to fall back on her own resources and hold everything inside.

Recent studies and research in the field of psycho-neuro-immuno-endocrinology show that an inadequate maternal regulating function permanently influences immune capacities (Schore 1994). The severe urinary tract infection Sheila developed could be a somatic expression of feeling abandoned at a developmental stage when her coping mechanisms were inadequate to deal satisfactorily with her affective needs. Her attempts at doing without help from the maternal object are clearly observable, as are her holding on to her distressed feelings and frustrations for an incredible length of time, given her age. The absence of a cry for help exhibits something like an "emotional reflux" in the psychic area comparable to the one in the urinary area.

This "heroic" behavior on Sheila's part, which aims at preserving the tenuous attachment with her maternal object, has created an omnipotent defense mechanism against her helplessness with disastrous repercussions to her physical health. The video is disturbing to watch insofar as it shows the baby's suffering in her isolation and helplessness. It also clearly shows that feeding needs to be a relational experience, not just the bottle, but the whole of the mother offering it.

One can look at Sheila's somatic disorder as a consequence of the failure of proper attachment and bonding, keeping in mind insecure-avoidant attachment as an aspect of clinical relevance (Bowlby 1969; 1973; 1981).

The situation can be extremely difficult for an infant when the mother is depressed, physically incapacitated, or emotionally disturbed. Even though she may be physically present, she cannot help the infant self to perform the regulation of archetypal affects. This lack can lead to serious psychosomatic disturbances in the child.

In summary, the real mother mediates the relationship between her baby and the innate archetypal drives, mitigating the absolute aspects, both good and bad, originally constellated at birth. Thus, the integration levels reached by the maternal ego, as well as the mother's unconscious processes, are of vital importance for the healthy psychic development of the infant. Experts on infancy from different perspectives have come to agree that the infant's emotional life develops in the context of a relationship both conscious and unconscious with the mother. Consequently, the mother's mental state, and unconscious representations or unconscious fantasies about her infant, influence the infant's experience more than does her conscious behavior.

The unconscious fantasies or mental representations that grip the personality of the mother are in a sphere outside her conscious awareness and therefore cannot be modified.

Another factor determining early emotional disturbances is located in the collective environment, the culture of a particular group or community. Thus it is unfortunate that our western culture does not support or facilitate early relationships. Because of a variety of factors the family/cultural situation and our "modern" lifestyle have deprived the infant–parent relationship of the protective nourishing environment necessary to support the early stages of human life.

Early disturbances and the psychosomatic patient

In the course of my work with many patients who presented severe psychosomatic symptoms I have come to the conclusion that early affects split off from ego consciousness and buried in the body were causing the patients to suffer pains and illnesses for which no physical cause could be detected.

I propose that the psychosomatic patient is forced to use, for lack of maternal reverie, his or her body or bodily organs (instead of the mother's mind) as a container and signifier, as a kind of stage upon which the unfelt psychic pain can be dramatized and eventually relieved.

Such patients in infancy were attended to by a mother whose mind was either disturbed or totally preoccupied with personal worries, rather than being attuned to her infant's emotional and physical states. For instance, the patient whom I will later describe in this chapter had a mother who suffered from bipolar disorder and who developed severe postpartum psychotic episodes lasting for several months following each childbirth.

The mothers of many of my other psychosomatic patients suffered from depression, had been hospitalized after childbirth, suffered addictions, or had to go back to work too soon. Thus, their infants' emotional needs were neglected. In such situations the body remains the container of pain as the mother does not help the infant differentiate between physical and emotional pain.

Pain that is made concretely visible in the body can be attended to and relieved by the mother or the environment (e.g. doctors), who understand suffering only in concrete terms. The somatic symptom becomes a dramatization of impalpable psychic pain.

In our collective culture pain is most often concretely understood as illness, whereas the emotionally distressed behavior of children is understood as "badness." Thus, both manifestations of psychic pain are misunderstood. Medication and surgery are prescribed for bodily organs which malfunction because of emotional stress, and punishment is applied to emotionally distressed children who display maladjusted behavior. It seems that the psychosomatic field is acted out in the culture, which operates like a mindless mother, one who is unable to process emotional distress as a factor precipitating the somatizations.

In Hannah's case (below), one could say that her body had become psychotic and was enacting her mother's mental illness, whereas Hannah appeared to be the best-adjusted, most competent, intelligent, and responsible person possible since early childhood. She had even taken on the mothering role, having helped her father like a good little surrogate wife and attended with great dedication to her many disturbed acting-out little brothers. She was the nurse in charge of her mentally ill mother in between hospitalizations. In short, her behavior was perfect, but her body kept falling apart under the huge emotional pressures she was made to carry. As many "good girls" do, she became self-sacrificing and totally dedicated to the well-being of others. Her aggressive and negative elements, which could find neither outlet nor containment in her environment or in an adult mind that could help her make sense of them, became relegated to her body and made it ill. Unlike the archetype of the hero, which makes the young man act out his violence against the "bad guys" out there, the heroine turns the aggression against herself and attacks her own body.

Hannah

Hannah, an attractive woman in her late thirties, was referred to me by a colleague who knew of my interest in early traumas. She had had several years of psychoanalytic therapy which had helped her somewhat but had not managed to reach the root of her problems which she knew were related to her infancy and her mother's postpartum psychosis and hospitalization.

Her mother's breakdown first occurred when Hannah was eighteen months; the mother required hospitalization when Hannah was two and was hospitalized for a year. During that time, Hannah was placed in a children's home during the day. Her father took her home on weekends and took care of her as best he could. She was extremely attached to her father, who on the one hand tried to do all he could for her, and on the other submitted her to herculean tasks. He did not seem to recognize his daughter's actual emotional capacity and was unable to relate to her emotional distress. He behaved as if his wife were normal and as if her hospitalizations were minor occurrences. Hannah was supposed to deal with them as part of everyday life as he had enough to do to work and provide for his large family and his sick wife.

The family was of German Lutheran origin, which explains some of the father's dutiful, rigid mentality and the superegoic behavior he imposed on his daughter. He seems to have felt ashamed of his wife's mental state and hid it from friends and neighbors. He forbade Hannah to complain about the family problems to anyone outside the family.

The two other members of the family were the paternal grandparents. Hannah was very attached to the grandmother, who seemed to help her in many practical ways. The grandfather was prone to drink and sexually abused Hannah and her younger brothers when left to babysit them.

At school Hannah was a brilliant student. The teachers, who were mostly concerned with academic achievement, never seemed to think about her emotional state.

Her ability to comply and her ego defense mechanisms were unusual. She operated by denial, splitting, and complying – but her somatizations were unending. Of course, the advantage of becoming physically ill is that, at the risk of one's own survival, one manages temporarily to relieve emotional pressure and to receive some care and a space within which to regress, be it hospital or convalescent home.

Hannah's analysis

Hannah had difficulty in agreeing to come to analysis three times a week. She was well educated in Jungian psychology and was studying for a Ph.D. in management and conflict-resolution. She told me she had to resolve a situation with an ex-boyfriend and decide what to do with her Ph.D. program that was unsatisfying to her. She had also to decide where she wanted to live because she did not feel happy in Washington. She had been here for two years and had made no friends. She had a degree in law and had a good knowledge of financial issues, as she had been a bank manager for several years.

She was attractive, well groomed and dressed in a casual California style that suited her and made her look much younger than her age. She carried on a pleasant conversation and was able to define her problems, but her speech lacked appropriate affect.

She was the typical alexithymic patient described by Joyce McDougall. She reported abuses, medical misdiagnoses, and privations that she had suffered throughout her life in a matter-of-fact way, as if she were recounting someone else's story.

It was clear to me from the beginning that she had to split off the affective content for fear of what might happen. She might act crazy like her mother, and then she would have to be locked up. The only containing place had to be her body, and she kept herself stiffly in control of her every move.

My countertransference from the start was disbelief at the expectations her family had of her as a child, and outrage at her exploitation, which she continued to submit to. I found her superhuman niceness and lack of affect irritating. I also wondered how she could possibly still trust someone in the helping professions, having heard of all the previous mistreatment by doctors of her mother and herself.

Hannah had cared for her mother until she died, in spite of her madness and dangerous behavior; she had cared for three severely addicted brothers. She had obeyed the dictates of her tyrannical father as a dutiful daughter all her life. She had submitted herself to injuries that a number of insensitive and incompetent doctors had inflicted on her body. She had married two men who had abused her emotionally and physically, repeating in the marriages the pattern of her original relationships in the home.

I pointed out to her that she appeared programmed to self-denial and obedience as the archetypal sister of mercy, and that we would have great difficulty working with the defense mechanisms that had served her survival in childhood and were still operative.

I made many interpretations in this sense. She understood what I was aiming at, but kept saying she was unable to feel any annoyance. She knew that her previous therapy had helped her understand how angry she had felt at her mother, but her father's image was sheltered by a positive archetypal godlike projection and could not be stained.

I told her that it had been important for her as a child to make father super-good, to make sure that there was someone there she could rely on for the protection she so badly needed. However, it seemed to me that her submission and competence had allowed her father to exploit her. Slowly we were able to use the behavior of a professor and another male student who were both exploitative of her to make her understand how she had played into their power and control issues. When she realized that she had been exploited, she became furious and yet could be respected.

I said that she lacked an alliance with a strong mother to show her that being nice and polite ended with letting herself be exploited. With a lot of hard work on my part she was slowly able to use my support to put these two men in their place, feeling empowered by our analytic work.

I said that it was as if at last she had found a mother who could listen to her complaints and help her make things right. She began to trust that she could rely on me for help and kept bringing new issues that she found difficult to manage. This brought about distressing memories of how un-helped and lonely she had felt in her life, and some affect began to emerge.

At this point I warned her that we might be faced with some severe somatic disturbances such as she had exhibited in the past, and asked her to come four times a week for the time being. She slipped into the frame of more frequent sessions as into a longed-for but unimaginable comfort. She then told me about her difficulties with procrastination and her endless, mindless, addictive games of solitaire when she was at home alone, which kept her from making friends. She told me that in the same way that she could not give up solitaire, she could not stop seeing the ex-boyfriend who, she knew, was wasting her time and energy.

I was watching out for some physical symptoms to appear, and indeed she began to complain about backache. I told her that the conflict inside her between wanting to get away from him and not being able to do so was splitting her back in two.

I suggested she tell him she did not want to see him again and that he should leave her alone. As she managed to be firm with him, her backache improved and she was no longer paralyzed by the conflict.

Thus, I began to show her the way in which her bodily symptoms could be used to introduce her to her emotions and her conflicts. Slowly, as her work progressed, it was as if she needed a new lexicon to decode her body's messages and to re-enter the emotional area.

It is my hypothesis that emotions in psychosomatic patients have become foreclosed and forbidden in childhood and as a consequence the mother's containing function cannot be differentiated by either mother or infant. In Hannah's case the sudden early breakdown and disappearance of her mother created a rupture in her continuity of being. She must have felt lost and unable to communicate what she was feeling. She had to deal with distressed feelings by temporarily blurring her awareness of their existence by clinging to factuality.

It appeared to me that in Hannah the link between the instinctual pole of the experience and its mental representation had been broken and/or had never been established. Thus the archaic proto-images had remained buried or encapsulated in the unconscious pole of the archetype. Not having been named by the mother, they had remained silent, unarticulated, and had no access to preconscious or conscious thought or dreams. In fact, Hannah had hardly any dreams and the dreams she did have had only factual content. She had a brilliant intellect but little fantasy material or imagination. It was as if she had to squash her imagination for fear that it could run wild and take her to places inside herself which she needed to avoid.

Such a patient poses a technical problem. The analyst must pay a great deal of attention to subliminal messages conveyed by the body and much less attention to the verbal, factual report. The unintegrated emotional fragments are located in the body. Thus, one must listen with a "third ear" and observe with a "third eye" to detect minute nuances that are extremely important communications but that the patient presents as irrelevant.

My countertransference with these patients is rooted in my experience and most of all in my experience of observing young infants and their nonverbal way of relating. Once I enter the pre-oedipal area of relationship I have to work my way towards making the hopeless infant inside the patient trust that I am there and am genuinely interested and caring about his or her struggle to survive.

In that way, when the attachment sets in, the patient will slowly use me to make up for the mirroring experience he or she missed in infancy. The most important part of the work is in establishing an emotional container into which the patient can project his or her unmetabolized experiences and have the analyst process them.

In this sense, although these patients present a very developed and competent façade, their symbolic processes are not yet plugged in. Therefore, the analytic work has to stay very close to earth to avoid the patient's becoming inflated as a defense against psychic pain. It is only after the bodily symptoms have disappeared and the area of psychic pain has been reached that analysis proper can take place.

It has been said that psychosomatic patients are unanalyzable. I disagree with this statement. In my long experience of working with these patients I have come to believe that analysis can be done, but only after the meaning has been extracted from the physical symptom and redirected into the psychic field.

Chapter 8

When the meaning gets lost in the body

In this chapter I will explore severe physical symptoms exhibited by patients at crucial stages of their analysis, which tend to occur when a "big change" is foretold in dreams or following interpretive work aimed at providing the patient with insight into his or her major psychic conflict.

My hypothesis is that, for some patients, when an interpretation manages to break through into a primitive deeply unconscious area, while the patient's ego struggles to gain psychological insight, the core of the personality offers extreme resistance to letting the infantile contents acquire a symbolic mental representation. In these patients, severe somatization occurs. The newly emerging insight appears to be too much for the patient's psyche to deal with.

The upsurge of affect reaches the threshold of the "zone of meaning," appears to short-circuit it and to discharge itself into the body or into bodily organs. Thus, the body provides the last bulwark against integration.

These primitive unconscious affective contents which I have observed refer to early life-threatening experiences which were defended against by extreme splitting.

My hypothesis is that the primitive affects, brought about by certain experiences in infancy, were not attributed any psychic meaning by the mother. That is to say, the mother had not been able to process the excess of affective contents for her infant because she was either emotionally disturbed or absent, whether emotionally or physically.

In the course of my analytic experience, I have noticed that patients who react somatically, children and adults alike, are generally very gifted people who, at the beginning of analysis, exhibit strong ego defenses. These have allowed the patients to function well in certain areas of their personality, in spite of an extremely primitive core in which archetypal affects predominate, encapsulated by defenses of the self.

Michael Fordham hypothesized that defenses of the self are the earliest defenses which are mobilized within the primary self of the infant. They function as a total defensive system for the purpose of survival when the mother fails to provide basic emotional care and the infant is exposed to survival panic and dread. These early undigested contents are not, as one might expect, ejected by these patients by means of a violent psychotic episode or psychic regressive breakdown. Rather, in some mysterious way, they enter the somatic sphere and get lost in the meanders of the body, producing violent physical reactions rather than being transformed into mental images or fantasies that could then be assimilated further.

My observation is that such patients do produce archetypal images, but these are disaffected (as in the case of alexithymia). These patients are emotionally detached observers of their own images. They defend themselves against feeling the horror, panic, and despair evoked by the archetypal image in relation to their own personal experience, and tend to view the image as an artistic creation. In these patients, archetypal primitive areas have been split off from their otherwise often well developed personality. Their emotional memory has been lost in the archaic somatic memory of the body, used as a storehouse.

Jung's theory of the bipolarity of the archetypes

My hypothesis is consistent with Jung's theory of the archetypes as unconscious entities having two poles, the one expressing itself in instinctual impulses and drives, the other in the form of fantasies.

My speculation is that, in the patient prone to somatization, the two polarities of the archetypal experience have been split into two distinct halves: the body and the psyche. The instinctual part has remained lodged in the body and the spiritual part has become an empty image.

From the exploration of the personal history of these patients it emerged that they all had experienced early emotionally disturbed or traumatic relationships with their mothers, who had been unable to mediate violent archetypal affective discharges in their infants. These shortcomings did not allow for the bodily archetypal experience to acquire stable mental representation in the sense Jung meant when he wrote that the image represents the meaning of the instinct (1947: 201).

The transcendent function and symbolic functioning

Jung wrote: "The shuttling to and fro of arguments and affects represents the transcendent function of opposites. The confrontation of the two positions generates a tension charged with energy and creates a living, third thing . . . a new situation" (Jung 1957a: 90). I would add, "whenever there is sufficient consciousness to be able to imagine a new situation."

Jung again:

> The transcendent function manifests itself as a quality of conjoined opposites. So long as these are kept apart – naturally for the purpose of avoiding conflict – they do not function and remain inert. In whatever form the opposites appear in the individual, at bottom it is always a matter of a consciousness lost and obstinately stuck in one-sidedness, confronted with the image of instinctive wholeness and freedom.
>
> (Jung 1957a: 90)

Here Jung tends to idealize instinctive wholeness, equating it with freedom. However, we know from observation and knowledge of infancy – which is the most instinctive stage of human life – that instinctive wholeness is the opposite of freedom. It is overwhelming, unthinkable, and uncontainable in the human mind.

Jung's image of the archaic man may be misleading, and it risks becoming romanticized and disconnected from the individual realm of experience. Thus, while he appears to value the compensatory function of the unconscious, which constellates the "archaic man," in the very same paper he warns against the dangers of the "ego of the rediscovered unconscious."

One is here alerted to Jung's fear of his own unconscious instinctual contents, because his language is heavily loaded with superegoic terms. He seems to alternate between depicting "consciousness" as a rigidly defended ego which is split from "instinctive wholeness," while at the same time advocating a flexible ego which would be able to integrate conflicting opposites.

The point to emphasize here is that Jung does not describe ego-consciousness structuring within the context of a dyadic relationship. It seems to occur in a state of isolation, where the ego has to "win" its own battle against the monsters of the archetypal world, or succumb. Jung seems to be describing his own lonely quest, guided by his superego mercilessly driving the ego, rather than by a flesh-and-blood mother who could experience mercy for his strivings. At the same time, by taking a moralistic position, Jung seems to contradict his own theory of the heuristic value of the unconscious.

Fordham's contribution to new developments in Jungian theory

By conceptualizing the primary self (the self at the beginning of life) as a psychosomatic unity, a sort of blueprint on which conscious and unconscious will become differentiated by the deintegrative/reintegrative dynamisms of the self promoted by archetypal activity, Michael Fordham has opened a new way to understand early and regressed psychic phenomena.

The primary self deintegrates immediately after birth (or even before). That is to say, it opens up towards the environment in order to meet the object which will satisfy its archetypal expectations. It then reintegrates by going back into itself in order to assimilate and digest that experience.

This dynamic occurs according to individual rhythms over and over again, and presupposes the expectation of an object which will provide satisfaction: the mother.

The value of this view is that it stresses the archetypal expectation of a relationship which then embodies itself in the mother–infant dyadic relationship.

Thus, we have to presuppose two archetypally determined concomitant dynamisms: the deintegration–reintegration of the primary self, and the to-and-fro of communication within the nursing couple. In this sense, the concept of archetypes is helpful, since it refers to innate patterns of behavior with mental concomitants.

Let us now apply Jung's concept of the transcendent function and embody it into the metaphor of the mother–infant couple where the "shuttling to and fro of arguments and affects" has to be imagined in a two-body relationship model rather than in the lonely "heroic one." According to this vertex, the "tension charged with energy [generated by the confrontation] creates a living thing."

I would call this "emotional relatedness." Symbolic creations develop within the relationship, metaphorically used as a stage where the interplay of the opposites can be safely experienced. According to Winnicott, "symbolic play" occurs when one is able to be "alone in the presence of another."

If we then assume that, under normal circumstances, the mother helps the infant make sense of the world and of itself, we can picture growth of consciousness as a process taking place within the container of the dyadic relationship.

However, certain mothers – because of their own disturbances – behave addictively toward their babies. They cling to them as if to a part of themselves, which they cannot let go of, for fear of a catastrophic mutilation. These mothers split off highly charged unconscious contents which their own psyches cannot bear.

As a result, these emotions and thoughts become totally foreclosed and forbidden to their child. In the same way, bodily zones or physiological functions disavowed by the mother become forbidden and disaffected for the child, in order to prevent a tearing apart of the mother–baby link. As a consequence, the dual aspect (both physical and emotional) of the mother's containing function cannot be differentiated by mother or infant alike.

Psychosomatic states and solutions

In her book *Theatres of the Body*, Joyce McDougall writes:

> In psychosomatic manifestations, the physical damage is real and the symptoms do not appear to reveal either a neurotic or a psychotic story. The "meaning" is of a presymbolic order that circumvents the use of words. In psychosomatic states the *body* appears to be behaving in a "delusional" fashion . . . . One is tempted to say that the body has gone mad.
>
> (McDougall 1989: 18)

McDougall hypothesizes that somatic expressions tend to arise in place of unrecognized psychotic fears and wishes. She adds to the classic somatic disorders (asthma, gastric ulcer, colitis, respiratory tract infections, arthritis, neurodermatitis) all cases of physical damage or illness in which psychological factors play an important role – accident-proneness, lowering of immunological shield, problems of addiction. She sees them as attempts to deal with distressing conflicts by temporarily blurring the awareness of their existence by clinging to factuality.

It appears that psychosomatic patients lack fantasies. In them the link between the instinctual pole of the experience and its mental representation has been broken, or never established. Thus, the proto-images – as archaic proto-fantasy/bodily elements – have remained buried or encapsulated in the unconscious bodily pole of the archetype. Not having been given a name by the mother, they have remained silent, are inarticulate, and have no access to preconscious or conscious thought or dreams.

I will now introduce three patients, two women and one child, each of whom has shown a dramatic tendency to somatize in the course of their analyses. Two of them were in three- or four-times-per-week analysis and the third in once-a-week analytic psychotherapy.

Ronnie: the cold feeling of separation

Ronnie used his bronchi as containers for the bad stuff he had accumulated in the early days of his life. He was three when he was referred to me. Ronnie was a highly intelligent and verbal child who presented a variety of neurotic symptoms at the stage of separating from his mother, such as nightmares, clinging behavior, and phobias.

He was born two months premature and spent the first two weeks of life in an incubator, where he had been severely ill with pneumonia and close to death. I have written about this case in *The Unfolding Self* and will mention here just one dramatic episode in the course of his analysis.

That episode occurred right after a meeting I had with his parents, which had made him very anxious. At the next session Ronnie complained bitterly about his parents' badness; he accused me too and told me he did not want to come back to see me any more. That session was followed by several others during which he refused to enter the room without his mother. Then he eventually became ill so he could not come at all. He remained absent for four weeks, suffering from bad bronchitis and severe respiratory tract infection. Analysis was impossible. His parents were worried, because the antibiotics did not seem to work.

I understood his somatization as both a regression to his early days in the incubator, and as a way of dealing with his rage which would be acceptable to his family, i.e. being ill. They could both comfort him and remove him from my presence, which was causing him so much upset.

Following his illness, I had to be absent for a week. When he came back, we had to work through a strong negative transference. He wanted to shoot me and bite me, and occasionally he managed to hit me hard. I withstood these attacks and talked to him about his feelings about my not visiting him when he was sick, which made him feel as he did soon after birth, that is to say abandoned by his mother, unprotected in the hospital where the bad doctors were torturing him.

In response to my interpretation he started coughing and carried on coughing for a long time. He looked very miserable, so I commented that he felt bad and that, like the doctors, I was making him feel worse. After my comment, he stopped coughing and went back to playing. The following session he was well again. He came into the session pretending to carry a baby horse in his hands. He told me the horse had been born at the time he had started analysis and that he was ill with a bad cough now. He built what looked like an incubator (a warm, womb-like place) and told me that the horse had to stay there and keep warm until he recovered. He took great care of the horse and talked to it. He eventually said that the horse was better now and left the session in a very good mood.

In the course of this severe somatization Ronnie had managed to regress to his dreadful infantile experience which I could contain in my mind and empathize with.

Thanks to the analytic work, the elements that had not acquired a mental form but were communicated by the body as a replay of his early catastrophic (near-death) experience found a symbolic expression. After this severe somatization his tendency to somatize improved dramatically.

Mary and the cast armor

Mary was in her late thirties when she came to me for therapy. From the recounting of her early history I expected the transference to constellate her early deprivation, and I wondered whether she would be able to tolerate the frustration and pain that it would bring about in such a loose analytic timeframe. On the other hand, she was lively, bright, and determined, which encouraged me to take her on. She needed three- or four-times-weekly analysis but could manage to come only once a week. This limited attendance created a real difficulty, which I knew would make her psychological work extremely hard. We talked about the difficulties the treatment would bring about. She seemed ready to take these on as a challenge to her heroic side, and she did not appear to be discouraged.

She was working with adolescents as a school counselor. She had brought up a child on her own and had been married and divorced more than once. She told me that she wanted to understand her moods and her deep feelings of worthlessness. Her bodily posture struck me from the beginning; I fantasized that she was wearing a rigid corset. She was of medium height and had an interesting face with expressive eyes and an attractive smile.

She told me that when she was eleven weeks old her mother, who was pregnant again, was hospitalized for a long time due to a life-threatening ulcerative colitis. Mary and her two older sisters were left to the care of her father and maternal grandmother. At first, she was unable to connect the feelings caused in her infant self by the dramatic separation and illness of her mother to her fears and difficulties in the present.

In the transference, she exhibited a fear of emotional closeness for which she compensated with a desperate search for physical intimacy in love relationships which usually turned into sadomasochistic ones.

It felt to me that being in therapy only once weekly was a torture for her infantile needs, but she could not let herself acknowledge it. She denied any difficulties and seemed to feel that my insistence on the matter was having a rather smothering effect on her.

In the countertransference I was aware of her frustration and I interpreted it to her, but to no avail. I often felt concerned by her acting out, which I could only contain from a distance, or would hear about afterwards. I felt anxious and impotent. The feelings I was experiencing referred to her infantile emotional state when her mother had left her. I had to hold onto them for her for a long time because they were unreachable to her.

It took a long time for me to help her try to reconnect her early dramatic experiences with the split-off affects related to them. She talked about severe scoliosis, for which she had a spine operation and had to wear a cast throughout her adolescence. At first she talked about her sufferings in a factual way, as if she were giving a medical history to a doctor. I wondered what it must have felt like for her to be confined in such a way during most of her adolescence. How much fear, pain, anxiety, and feelings of inferiority and worthlessness she must have experienced, while the other teenagers, her siblings included, could participate in sports and enjoy themselves.

A tremendously ambivalent love/hate relationship with her younger brother emerged in the course of the sessions. She admitted that she had felt responsible for her brother's unhappiness, remembering that she had wished to get rid of him who in reality had been the cause of her mother's illness.

In fantasy, however, at a much deeper level, she blamed her mother's hospitalization on her own infant greed and demands. In the transference she was extremely attentive not to demand anything from me for fear that I would become sick and abandon her too. A couple of sessions I arrived late at our appointment; despite my attempts to reach her obvious annoyance and anger, she kept reassuring me that it was all right and that these things could happen! She would become very understanding, making excuses to protect me, terrified as she was to feel any negative feelings toward me.

Not long before coming to therapy, her brother, a professional skier, had been caught in an avalanche and had lost one leg. Mary had been totally devastated by his mutilation. During our sessions we were finally able to explore the unconscious feelings of hostility and rivalry she harbored towards him.

In the second year of her therapy, we focused on her back problem. She took up martial arts and worked just as seriously in making her body flexible as she applied herself to gaining insight into her psychic conflicts.

At breaks she denied her distress, but tended to develop a love relationship to fill the gap of my absences from her, as she had done at the time of her mother's illness by becoming attached to grandmother in order to survive. It took three years for her to be able to admit that she missed me during a therapy break.

Soon after my return, some forgotten memories of her childhood surfaced, together with feelings of distress which she had previously fended off. I felt that the early defenses against the pain of the catastrophic separation in infancy had started to give way.

Then she fell ill with severe bronchitis, high fever, and pains in her chest which lasted for several weeks and resisted treatment. During her illness she could not come to therapy and she experienced the depth of her misery and abandonment, coupled with fear of dying, just like in her adolescence when her back was operated on.

At the first session following her sickness she told me that she felt weak, lost, confused, and frightened, but that she could not put into words what her fear was about. I asked her to try to give it a name. The following week she returned feeling much better. "I have thought about it," she said immediately, "the name which came up is 'death.'"

We began to explore her terror, and it emerged that the day on which she fell ill had been the anniversary of her operation. For the first time, twenty-eight years later, she was able once again to feel the panic and terror she had denied and repressed in the past. "It was awfully painful and I could not move. That same day John Kennedy was shot, and everybody was preoccupied with the news. He was more important than my pain."

She went on to describe how much she had been in pain and added out of the blue, "You know, my aunt had died of the same operation because of a mistake of the surgeon a few months earlier. We all knew about it, but both my parents and I blocked it at the time." The horror of her aunt's death had reawakened the early panic and dread experience at the time of her mother's hospitalization. Neither one of these emotions had ever been connected to Mary's operation by her parents, and the dread and panic related to both experiences had remained unnamed, a silent event in her life which had no access to her consciousness but which was dramatized by the body.

Elizabeth and the cold envelope: the skin as a container

Elizabeth was in her mid-thirties when she came to see me. She was feeling disconnected from the reality of her present life in a foreign country, which she experienced as cold and rejecting. She had three children of whom she was extremely proud, but her marriage was on the rocks.

Elizabeth was a real blue-blood aristocrat. Attractive and distinguished, controlled and extremely cold, she had a superior and somewhat arrogant attitude towards me, a person who needed to work for her living, much as the nanny of her childhood.

It soon emerged that her beautiful and gifted mother, who lived in the family castle, was a severe alcoholic. Elizabeth felt guilty for not being able to tolerate her mother's behavior and for being unable to help her.

She had had a troubled childhood, always having to attend to her alcoholic mother. She was nine years old when her parents divorced. Her father basically abandoned her, leaving her in charge of the family and of her three younger brothers, as she put it. She resented it, but loved and respected her father none the less.

It was difficult to establish and maintain a solid analytic frame with Elizabeth because, although I managed to have her come three times a week, she was terrified to enter into a close relationship with me, let alone be analyzed. She used her family or social commitments as excuses to manipulate her analytic frame. I had to be very firm, interpreting her terror both of attachment and of closeness. It seemed to me that she dreaded to find herself once again dependent on an addictive mother/analyst who would destroy her. She lay stiffly on the couch, talking with a monotonous affected tone of voice, and she kept my interpretations at arm's length.

She would report with no emotion excruciatingly painful episodes of her childhood and her perverse sexual relationship with her husband. Also, her dreams contained primitive psychotic material which she reported in a disaffected way.

She had suffered from anorexia for some years in her early twenties, but had received no treatment. She admitted that she had felt very unattractive as a young girl compared to her beautiful mother, who had many admirers. She had married her present husband, who was the son of her mother's second husband, more to compete with her mother than because she was in love with him. After some years she had had an affair with one of her husband's relatives. The secret affair ended quickly and made her feel dirty, guilty, and in need of expiation. She turned to religious practices and devoted herself, as a penance, to her family and her husband, who by then had started to treat her badly and was degrading her.

When her husband announced that he wanted a divorce, she became severely ill with kidney failure and nearly died. She took her husband's rejection as a punishment for her infidelity and persevered in holding on to him, accepting degrading and verbally abusive behavior on his part.

Such was the situation when she came to see me. Almost every night she dreamed that her husband had been killed, or was being tortured, or that she had been cut open and that her body was bleeding to death.

While all this was going on in her inner world, outwardly she appeared very composed, detached, and unaffected. She had studied art and had an interest in painting and architectural design, for which she was gifted. Her dreams were full of images which were only to be looked at, but not to be touched by me. The only area she allowed me to touch and to work on was that of her relationship with her children, an area in which she felt fairly comfortable. Then I used her children's feelings to start introducing her internal child and her feelings. Slowly she began to talk about her lonely childhood in the company of servants. Her parents were seldom available. They went to many social functions and only occasionally would they drop by the nursery at bedtime to see the children. She behaved well in the sessions, as her parents had expected her to do in childhood.

In the second year of her analysis, while working on the issue of separation from her husband and her mother, her mother suddenly died of an overdose. Elizabeth felt both overwhelmed by guilt and strangely relieved. She did not shed a tear, but immediately developed severe eczema on her hands and face. Scales, like that of a cold-blooded reptile, covered her skin. She scratched herself and her hands were bleeding and painful. She remembered having had the same eczema as a baby when, at the age of twelve months, her parents had left her to go on a cruise and had been away for three months. At that time she had to be tied to the bed because she scratched herself so badly and cried desolately all night.

In the countertransference, I felt warmly towards her suffering, but she rejected my empathic feelings, and I was not allowed to get close to her emotionally or to touch her little child's feelings with warm comforting words. She hardened up and rejected my concern as being sentimental and weak. She remained isolated by her eczema and the "envelope of cold" unrelatedness, as if allowing me to touch her emotionally would have meant melting away in unbearable pain, confusing herself with her own mother's unspeakable despair.

She could not begin to cry for fear of being overwhelmed by her despair, for which there had never been a container other than her own skin. But now, under the pressure of the horrible pain, her skin, the last container, had cracked too, and she was terrified to let go.

She decided that she needed to salvage her mother's memory by organizing an exhibition of her work in her hometown in order to have, as she put it, "something good to remember," both for herself and for the world. The exhibition was a success and this allowed her to feel as if she had concretely made reparation. This made her feel more contained and in charge of herself. Her eczema improved and slowly disappeared.

She decided to divorce her husband, took a course in design, and eventually told me that she was going to go back to her mother's town. She dismissed me as a servant no longer needed.

She left without thanks and without showing any distress. I felt bad and left in the cold but felt sure that I would see her again.

A year later she contacted me. She was softer, mellower, and spoke in a warmer tone of voice. She told me that as soon as she arrived at her mother's house she had experienced an uncontainable need to cry. Tears had burst out of her eyes and she had sobbed for week after week until, as she said, she had cried all her tears. Now at last she was also able to tell me that she had missed me, and she acknowledged how much the work she had done with me had helped her. The tears had burst out as an appropriate expression of her pain. In the past, the eczema had expressed her pain in a nonverbal way, because her baby self had felt that her crying was unbearable to her mother. She had to leave me to feel safe enough to let her pain surface. If she had stayed, she feared that, like the mother of her childhood, I would have engulfed her in my bottomless distress.

The envelop of cold, superior disdain and disaffection had melted away and she had become a real flesh-and-blood human being who could experience pain and withstand it.

Discussion

The body as container and signifier

I propose that the psychosomatic patient uses his or her own body or bodily organs (instead of the mother's mind) as a container and signifier, as a kind of stage upon which psychic pain can be dramatized and eventually relieved. The *body* becomes the *container* of pain, undifferentiated but concretely visible because as such it is attended to and relieved by a mother who understands suffering only in concrete terms. There is no room for invisible, impalpable psychic pain. The somatic symptom becomes an expression, a dramatization of psychic pain which has the quality of a mime rather than a play. It is a drama without words, through which the body of the sufferer will receive the primary care that will vicariously provide solace and comfort to the soul.

I have observed that somatic patients come from families where pain is concretely understood as illness. In the course of infant observation seminars I have noticed that, in families where the mother is unable to use imaginative or abstract language and where she denies imagination and fantasies, babies learn to avail themselves of the body, and of words referring to fact, to communicate with the mother.

The way in which I use the idea of the body as container is somewhat different from Bovensiepen's "body as containing object." He describes adolescent patients who deal with their bodies in aggressive, self-destructive, mutilating ways, but who have fantasies about it and who seem to know, however dimly, what they are doing to their bodies, although they ignore why they are doing it. They seem to be stating, "This body is mine and I will do with it whatever I like."

In the psychosomatic patient, the bodily organ takes over, and the patient is totally unaware of what is going on. In the course of analysis, when the integrative process is set in motion, due to analytically gained insight, somatization occurs as a specific form of acting out.

Technical problems in working with psychosomatic patients

It has been observed in infant observation seminars that some babies exhibit strong egos from birth and are apparently able to tolerate extremely distressing situations without crying or protesting although they are falling apart. These we call "helpful babies," as they appear to want to parent and protect the mother. They seem to understand the mother's fragility and behave in a supportive way, but we have noticed that from early on they show a tendency to somatize. They become ill and require maternal concern exclusively for their physical conditions, rather than for emotional states with which the mother cannot help them.

When these patients come to analysis and the integrative process begins to be set in motion, severe somatizations often occur, which may cause serious anxieties and concerns in the analyst. This state of affairs (often very dangerous for the patient's survival) is also difficult for the analyst to bear and weather without being drawn into action. Rather than being concerned exclusively for their physical conditions, the analyst must maintain an impeccable analytic attitude.

I have connected this tendency to somatize with a lack in the development of the transcendent function. During these dark times for the patient, the transcendent function has to operate in the analyst, who will then be able to perform the maternal reverie that the original mother was unable to do for the patient as an infant. The major difficulty is a technical one: how to reach out and touch the patient with words rather than concretely. The interpretation in these cases has to aim at re-establishing the broken link between body and affects; in other words, exactly the opposite of what happened in the patient's infancy, where this link was severed.

In order to obtain this result, it is extremely important to use words suggesting concrete images of affects. For instance, when a patient talks about illness in terms of cold and cough, the analyst can comment about "the cold feeling and the bad stuff inside related to the experience of having been left out in the cold by an icy cold mother who made him feel cold and lonely." In this way, one attempts to provide the patient with imaginative language where affective and emotional elements can re-enter the body and the inner and outer experience will eventually be allowed to co-exist.

In cases when the analyst relinquishes the analytic attitude and is drawn into action by responding to the patient's body demands (by acting out sexually or in any other way), the analyst is repeating the early mother's behavior, that is to say not attending to the patient's emotional need and pain. Thus, the patient's potential for symbolic development is lost once again and may be permanently impaired.

All three patients in this chapter tried very hard to make me act out, by making me feel deeply troubled about their sufferings. All had experienced panic and dread as infants to an unusually high degree, and these feelings could not reach consciousness as they were concretely stuck in an organ where they produced physical pain. On my part I had to contain and process their panic and dread and could not act out in a pseudo-comforting way to soothe my distressed feelings.

Conclusion

This book contains portions of my life's work as an analyst. My work has been inspired and informed by Jung's theory of the self and the archetypes, which Fordham amplified and applied to infancy and childhood. Jung's concepts of the affects and the transcendent function, together with Fordham's concepts of the primary self and the deintegration–reintegration processes, underpin my analytic methodology as well as the infant observation seminars I developed and taught. Klein, Bion, Winnicott, McDougall, and others have also influenced me. Over the years I have developed my own way of working with child and adult patients, and it is my hope that the clinical material in this book has illustrated my theoretical stance and my particular method of conducting an analysis.

My interest has been to demonstrate how primary affects contribute to archetypal imagery and how the archetypal imagery constellated in early life can permanently influence a person's psychology.

Generally, I have delved deeply into the special psychological problems caused by early traumatic experiences of the infant and young child – illness, hospitalization, separation from the mother, misattunement with the mother, abandonment. These unfortunate circumstances lead to severe pathology in the child and adult. My particular concern has been for the person who suffered early trauma without the benefit of a maternal container who could make sense of the child's suffering by putting the situation into symbolic form, using thoughts and words.

Lacking meaning, the traumatic experiences often become lodged in the body, and the body expresses them. My task as an analyst has been to translate the message of the body and to help the patient make sense of his or her early experience in a symbolic way.

My goal has been to help the patient find the meaning hidden in, but spoken by, the body, so that trauma can be managed by the psyche. To achieve that goal, I have attempted to name what has previously been nameless.

My clinical material has ranged from that of very young infants observed in the course of the seminars I taught to the analysis of an aging adult.

I have used examples of children who exhibit bizarre symptomatology, who were brought to me with a diagnosis of autism or of attention deficit hyperactivity disorder. I have demonstrated how I reach beyond the symptom to the infant self of the patient, to contain it, and to interpret its suffering, bringing the child into a related experience, both with me and with his or her psychological issue. My particular emphasis has been to humanize archetypal experiences for the child.

I also have described my work with adolescents, showing how my symbolic method worked to stop acting-out behavior.

Further I have demonstrated in case material drawn from the analyses of psychosomatic adult patients how I related bodily symptoms to early traumatic experiences, so that the patient could develop a symbolic attitude, thus conquering psychic distress disguised as physical illness.

The theory underpinning my work has been clarified and enriched by these and other examples from case material. Now I would like to dwell on the analytic setting and say something about what being an analyst means to me.

Patients young and old come to therapy because they are stuck in some complex. They would like a change to occur, but often they do not know who or what should change and are afraid of it.

My rule is to let the patient speak. The problem will surface in the course of a couple of interviews. Then I make an interpretation directed to the core of the complex and await the patient's reactions. This intervention usually self-selects the future patient, and screens out the unsuitable ones.

Although analysis aims at freeing the personality, it is a hard and painful treatment requiring a great commitment, patience, the ability to tolerate frustration, and interest in the truth about oneself.

In our first meeting I tell all this to the patient, add my rules for conducting an analysis, and let the patient decide. Those who come back are usually ready to start. I like to see patients three times per week or more, but I try to address each individual's need for containment by increasing or decreasing the number of sessions.

Containment is an essential part of analysis. As analysis starts, so does regression induced by the transference of early pathological unconscious material. This is why containment is absolutely necessary to prevent acting out such as suicide or somatic reactions. The frame of analysis is an important element of containment. The external frame has been much emphasized, but in my view the analyst's internal disposition is more important and has not been stressed enough. The Jungian analyst Kenneth Lambert defined it as *agape* (Lambert 1981). That is to say, in order for an analysis to proceed, it is necessary that there be an ethical attitude encompassing spiritual and moral attributes in both analyst and patient. As Jung wrote, both analyst and patient are emotionally involved in the process and exposed to the danger of the unconscious (Jung 1956: 753).

Analysis is not a "cure," but rather a painful process of self-exploration and discovery aimed at freeing psychic energy blocked in complexes, which hopefully improves symptoms, but which more significantly allows the person to live a fuller life.

Analysis is dangerous. Dealing with the power of the archetypes requires knowledge, caution, and respect for the process. It is possible that the analyst may be caught in unconscious projections and act out. Therefore, an analyst must always be aware of his or her limits and, when in difficulty, must consult a colleague for supervision.

I know from experience that an analyst must be genuine and real in the relationship with the patient, unafraid to display emotions appropriate to the situation. In this way the patient will learn about appropriate emotions. I have learned that the patient's memories and narratives change dramatically as analysis progresses and therefore treat all the patient's communication as transference material for analysis, as I have demonstrated in the case material in this book.

The analyst's attitude should be non-judgmental and as free as possible from expectations; only this attitude will withstand the patient's testing attacks.

To conclude, an analyst's style will vary a great deal according to his or her personality, but the essentials are integrity, courage, love for the truth, patience, and the willingness to have one's own wounds reopened, to be as Jung said, a wounded healer.

Bibliography

Alvarez, A. (1992) *Live Company*, London: Tavistock/Routledge.

Anzieu, D. (1989) *The Skin Ego*, New Haven: Yale University Press.

Bion, W. (1967) *Second Thoughts*, London: Karnac.

Bion, W. (1970) *Attention and Interpretation*, London: Karnac.

Bion, W. (1988) *Learning from Experience*, London: Karnac.

Boston, M. and Szur, R. (eds) (1983) *Psychotherapy with Severely Deprived Children*, London: Routledge & Kegan Paul.

Bowlby, J. (1969) *Attachment*, London: Hogarth Press.

Bowlby, J. (1973) *Separation: Anxiety and Anger*, London: Hogarth Press.

Bowlby, J. (1981) *Loss: Sadness and Depression*, London: Hogarth Press.

Feldman, B. (1992) "Jung's Infancy and Childhood and Its Influence upon the Development of Analytical Psychology," *Journal of Analytical Psychology* 3/7: 255–76.

Fordham, M. (1973) "The Importance of Analysing Childhood for the Assimilation of the Shadow," in M. Fordham et al. (eds), *Analytical Psychology: A Modern Science*, Library of Analytical Psychology, 1, London: Karnac.

Fordham, M. (1976) *The Self and Autism*, London: Karnac.

Fordham, M. (1982) "Some Thoughts on Deintegration," (unpublished).

Fordham, M. (1985) "Countertransference," in *Explorations into the Self*, Library of Analytical Psychology, 7, London: Karnac.

Jung C. G. *Collected Works*, Princeton: Bollingen.

    (1921) "Definitions," in vol. 6.

    (1928) "On Psychic Energy," in vol. 8.

    (1934) "Archetypes of the Collective Unconscious," in vol. 9. i.

    (1938) "Psychological Aspects of the Mother Archetype," in vol. 9. i.

    (1939) "Conscious, Unconscious, and Individuation," in vol. 9. i.

    (1939) "The Concept of the Collective Unconscious," in vol. 9. i.

    (1947) "On the Nature of the Psyche," in vol. 8.

    (1951a) "The Psychology of the Child Archetype," in vol. 9. i.

    (1951b) "The Shadow," in vol. 9. ii.

    (1952) "Synchronicity: An Acausal Connecting Principle," in vol. 8.

(1954) "On the Tibetan Book of the Great Revelation," in vol. 11.
(1956) *Mysterium Coniunctionis*, vol. 14.
(1957a) "The Transcendent Function," in vol. 8.
(1957b) "The Undiscovered Self," in vol. 10.
Klein, M. (1988) *Envy and Gratitude and Other Works, 1946–1957*, London: Virago.
Lambert, K. (1981) *Analysis, Repair and Individuation*, London: Society of Analytical Psychology.
McDougall, J. (1989) *Theatres of the Body*, New York: Norton.
Piontelli, A. (1992) *From Fetus to Child: An Observational and Psychoanalytic Study*, London: Routledge, New Library of Psychoanalysis, vol. 15.
Piontelli, A. (1995) "Kin Recognition and Early Precursors of Attachment, As Seen in the Analysis of a Young Adopted Psychotic Boy," *Journal of Child Psychotherapy* 21/1: 5–21.
Redfearn, J. W. T. (1985) *My Self, My Many Selves*, London: Academic Press.
Schore, A. (1994) *Affect Regulation and the Origin of the Self*, Hillsdale: Lawrence Erlbaum Associates.
Sidoli, M. (1989) *The Unfolding Self*, Boston: Sigo Press.
Sidoli, M. (1995) "Oedipus as Preoedipal Hero," in M. Sidoli and G. Bovensiepen (eds), *Incest Fantasies and Self Destructive Acts*, New Brunswick: Transaction, 43–54.
Sidoli, M. and Davies, M. (eds) (1988) *Jungian Child Psychotherapy: Individuation in Childhood*, London: Karnac.
Stern, D. (1990) *Diary of a Baby*, New York: Basic Books.
Tomkins, S. (1962) *Affect/Imagery/Consciousness*, vol. 1: *The Positive Affects*, New York: Springer.
Tomkins, S. (1963) *Affect/Imagery/Consciousness*, vol. 2: *The Negative Affects*, New York: Springer.
Tustin, F. (1981) *Autistic States in Children*, London: Routledge & Kegan Paul.
Tustin, F. (1990) *The Protective Shell in Children and Adults*, London: Karnac.
von Franz, M.-L. (1970) *The Problem of the Puer Aeternus*, New York: Spring Publications.
Winnicott, D. W. (1971) *Playing and Reality*, London: Pelican Books.

Index

abandonment, feelings of 16–17, 44, 53, 57, 63, 68, 80, 95
absoluteness 35, 93
accident-proneness 107
acting out 2, 43–55, 110, 118; and collective shadow 73; and regression 64; somatization 115
adaptation 76
affect modulation (Schore) 89
affect-regulation 2, 94, 95–6
affective responses 74, 90
affects 8, 89, 90, 91; and birth 8, 15; bridge between body and psyche 1, 34, *see also* emotions
agape 119
alexithymia 99, 104
alienation 8
Alvarez, A. 81
ambivalence 64
analysis/analytic sessions: attachment 61, 102; mother-infant approach 18, 30; and non-verbal communication 52–3, 81, 101; painful process 119; positive identification 31; projection 12, 13, 20, 48–9; projective identification 63, 66, 69, 81, 83–4; reverie 30, 50, 55, 116; and somatization 100–1, 103, 108–9, 115, 116; transference 49–50, 63, 69, 79, 80, 108, 110, 118; working with shadow 78, *see also* countertransference; verbal interpretation
analyst: acting out 116; essential

characteristics of 119; role of 118–19
anger, inability to show 82, 83, 87, 100, 110–11
'animal tendencies' 76
anorexia 113
Anzieu, Didier 68
'archaic man' 105
archetypal affects 89, 90
archetypal drives 74
archetypal fantasies 11, 30, 56, 60, 81; collective 11; mother's 13–14; of self-fulfilment 75
archetypal field 23, 89–102
archetypal imagery 36, 74, 90–1; influence of 117; mythical 73; and primary affects 2, 117
archetypes 1, 33–4, 75, 89, 90, 117; bipolarity of 1, 34, 104; and birth 7–14; hero 16–17; observable in infancy 33; as organizers of experience 1, 33; positive and negative sides 33, 91
assimilation 36
attachment: failed 11, 95; fear of 112, 114
attention deficit hyperactivity disorder 118
autism 17–18, 118
autistic defenses 17–19, 21; working with 19–21, 23–31

bad mother archetype (bad breast) 2, 35, 37, 39, 92

beta elements 52, 60, 65, 92
Bion, W. 30, 52, 60, 65, 92, 117
birth: ambivalent feelings of parents
  9; and archetypal emotions 22–3;
  and archetypes 7–14; different
  cultural approaches to 22, 23;
  emotional space for infant 9; and
  emotions 7–9, 10, 15; expecta-
  tions/fantasies about 8–10; as
  medical event 7; premature 20–1,
  108; respiratory difficulties 21, 24,
  30, 57, 60; ritualistic meaning 7, 8
bodily symptoms: decoding 101, 118,
  see also physical symptoms;
  somatization
body: as container of pain 97, 98–9,
  100–1, 113–14, 115, 117; hidden
  meaning in 103–16, 117
bonding, insecure 11
Boston, Mary 69
Bovensiepen, G. 115

castration anxiety 50
'chaotic magma' 72
Child Analytical Training Program 32
child-rearing, collective beliefs about
  15
collective shadow 73–5; in analysis
  78, 81; and consciousness and
  unconscious 73–4; primitive
  content 73; and somatic illness 73,
  see also personal shadow; shadow
communication: breakthrough in
  69–70; non-verbal 52–3; through
  language 51–2
consciousness 36, 105; limits of
  potential 92
container/containment 29, 30, 59,
  68–9, 91, 102; need for 118–19;
  and pain 97, 98, 108, see also
  body; psychosomatic illness
countertransference 12, 46–7, 61,
  65–6, 79, 83, 101, 114; and autistic
  children 21; difficulties of 69–70,
  81; and interpretation 50, 66, 86, 110;
  usefulness of 52, 55, 63, 81, 85–6
creation myths 7

death, fear of 87, 111–12

death instinct 36
defense mechanisms 2, 48, 72, 75,
  76–7, 98, 100; and birth 8; during
  sessions 85, 87, see also splitting
'defense of the self' 17, 30, 56–70,
  75, 103–4
deintegration-reintegration 2, 10–12,
  30, 33, 41, 106; and maternal care
  3, 35–7, 69, 91, see also primary
  self
denial 2, 17, 80, 98
dependency, as negative experience
  75, 79
depressive position 64, 77
disintegration 30, 37, 38, 59, 69, 74,
  93–4; and post-partum depression
  11
dissociation 78
divine child archetype 84
doctors 15–16, 18, 19
dreams 80–1, 86–7, 88, 112, 113
dysfunctional interaction, and early
  intervention 42

eczema 43, 113
ego 36, 73; disintegration of 74;
  fragmentary 35; of the rediscovered
  unconscious 105; weakness of 73,
  75, see also psyche; self
ego function: development of 34–5,
  36, 90, 91; directed 76
ego-consciousness 90, 105
emotional container, establishing 102
emotional deprivation 56, 61, 64, 68,
  81
emotional relatedness 106
emotions 34; and body 72; and
  repression 77, see also affects
empathic attunement 22, 47, 91
encapsulation 17, 31, 38, 103, 108
enmeshment 17
evacuation 65, 69, 77
eye contact 23, 25

families, and alienation 8
farts/farting 56, 59, 60–1, 62, 64–5,
  68; as autistic objects 65; and
  countertransference 66; as
  defense of the self 65, 66, 68

self 1–2, 33, 92; and absoluteness 35;
as archetype of order 33; in infancy
93, 94; and interaction with
environmental 'mother/culture'
2–3; origin of 89; as totality of
psyche 1, 33, 89–90, 92, *see also*
ego; primary self; psyche
self-denigration 14
self-esteem 14, 53, 109, 110
self-sacrifice 97, 100
separation anxiety 57, 58
shadow 71–88; in analysis 78–88; and
body 72; collective 71, 73–7, 78,
81; and integration/assimilation 78;
personal 71, 76–7, 82, *see also*
collective shadow; personal
shadow
skin, as container 113–14
skin color, and rejection 13
smell 68
Society of Analytical Psychology,
London 32
soiling 58, 60–1
somatization 3; and bipolarity of
archetypes 104; during analysis
100–1, 103, 108–9, 115, 116,
see also psychosomatic illness,
body, as container
splitting 2, 47–8, 72, 75, 77, 78, 98,
103, 104
Stern, Daniel 93–4
suicide, unconscious fantasies of 43,
45, 47, 54

survival anxiety 73
symbolic functioning 105–6
symbolic thinking 51, 71, 74, 87, 94
synchronicity 89
syntony, between mother and child
processes 27–8, 30

toilet-training, resistance to 27
Tomkins, Sylvan 71
transcendent function 74–5, 105–6,
116
transformation 50, 56
Tustin, Frances 17–18

unconscious: compensatory function
of 105; and hero archetype 16;
heuristic value of 106
unpleasure principle 81

verbal interpretation 49–50, 62, 63,
66, 67, 83, 85–6, 100, 108–9, 116;
rejected by patient 49, 61, 65, 81,
110
'violent destructive' experiences 35
von Franz, Marie-Louise 84

Winnicott, D.W. 32, 61, 106, 117
witch archetype 39, 75, 82
withdrawal 17, 38
words, as autistic objects 45–6
wounded healer 119

'zone of meaning' 103